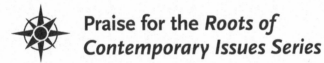

Praise for the *Roots of Contemporary Issues Series*

Everything around us—policy, population, culture, economy, environment— is a product of the actions and activities of people in the past. How can we hope to address the challenges we face and resolve contentious issues—like inequality, health, immigration, and climate change—without understanding where they come from? The volumes in the Roots of Contemporary Issues series are the tested products of years of classroom teaching and research. They address controversial issues with impartiality but not detachment, combining historical context and human agency to create accounts that are meaningful and usable for any student confronting the complex world in which they will live.

—TREVOR T. GETZ, *San Francisco State University*

This is a truly innovative series that promises to revolutionize how world history is taught, freeing students and faculty alike from the 'tyranny of coverage' often embedded within civilizational paradigms, and facilitating sustained reflection on the roots of the most pressing issues in our con- temporary world. Students' understanding of the importance of history and their interest in our discipline is sure to be heightened by these volumes that deeply contextualize and historicize current global problems.

—NICOLA FOOTE, *Arizona State University*

ROOTS OF CONTEMPORARY ISSUES

GENDER RULES

ROOTS OF CONTEMPORAY ISSUES

Series Editors

Jesse Spohnholz and Clif Stratton

The **Roots of Contemporary Issues** Series is built on the premise that students will be better at facing current and future challenges, no matter their major or career path, if they are capable of addressing controversial issues in mature, reasoned ways using evidence, critical thinking, and clear written and oral communication skills. To help students achieve these goals, each title in the Series argues that we need both an understanding of the ways in which humans have been interconnected with places around the world for decades and even centuries.

Ruptured Lives: Refugee Crises in Historical Perspective
Jesse Spohnholz, Washington State University

Power Politics: Carbon Energy in Historical Perspective
Clif Stratton, Washington State University

Chronic Disparities: Public Health in Historical Perspective
Sean Wempe, California State University, Bakersfield

Heavy Traffic: The Global Drug Trade in Historical Perspective
Ken Faunce, Washington State University

Gender Rules: Identity and Empire in Historical Perspective
Karen Phoenix, Washington State University

Gender Rules

Identity and Empire in Historical Perspective

Roots of Contemporary Issues

Karen Phoenix
Washington State University

New York   Oxford
OXFORD UNIVERSITY PRESS

Oxford University Press is a department of the University of Oxford.
It furthers the University's objective of excellence in research, scholarship,
and education by publishing worldwide. Oxford is a registered trade mark of
Oxford University Press in the UK and certain other countries.

Published in the United States of America by Oxford University Press
198 Madison Avenue, New York, NY 10016, United States of America.

For titles covered by Section 112 of the US Higher Education
Opportunity Act, please visit www.oup.com/us/he for the latest
information about pricing and alternate formats.

Library of Congress Cataloging-in-Publication Data

Names: Phoenix, Karen, author.
Title: Gender rules : identity and empire in historical perspective / Karen
    Phoenix, Washington State University.
Description: First Edition. | New York : Oxford University Press, 2020. |
    Series: Roots of contemporary issues | Includes bibliographical
    references and index. | Summary: "A higher education history text on
    gender rules in historical perspective"—Provided by publisher.
Identifiers: LCCN 2020028508 (print) | LCCN 2020028509 (ebook) | ISBN
    9780190696245 (paperback) | ISBN 9780197542798 (epub) | ISBN
    9780190696290
Subjects: LCSH: Sex role—History. | Gender identity—History.
Classification: LCC HQ1075 .P486 2020 (print) | LCC HQ1075 (ebook) | DDC
    305.309—dc23
LC record available at https://lccn.loc.gov/2020028508
LC ebook record available at https://lccn.loc.gov/2020028509

Printing number: 9 8 7 6 5 4 3 2 1
Printed by LSC Communications, Inc., United States of America

To my family, for their constant and unstinting support.

CONTENTS

LIST OF MAPS AND FIGURES

Maps

Figures

ABOUT THE AUTHOR

Karen Phoenix is Clinical Assistant Professor in the Roots of Contemporary Issues Program at Washington State University. She has over a decade of experience teaching American and world history, with thematic interests in gender, imperialism, and urbanization. Her research examines the United States in the World during the Progressive Era and interwar period, particularly focusing on issues of gender and cultural influence. This work has included exploring the US Young Women's Christian Association as a case study to exmine US attempts at cultural imperialism in India, the Philippines, Argentina, Nigeria, and Poland. She has published in the *Journal of the Gilded Age and Progressive Era*; *World History Connected*; and in the *The Routledge Handbook of Gender, War, and the US Military*. She has presented papers at national conferences such as the Berkshire Conference of Women Historians, the American Historical Association, and the Society for Historians of American Foreign Relations.

ACKNOWLEDGMENTS

Writing a book like this, which encompasses such a broad range chronologically and geographically, is a bit like trying to distill an ocean into a pint glass. It's an immense task that often feels too large to be accomplished, and can only be done with a crew of people to help along the way. I owe an immense debt to my fellow authors of the original works of this series—Jesse Spohnholz, Clif Stratton, Ken Faunce, and Sean Wempe—who served as sounding boards and gave me feedback as the various chapters of the book were taking shape. In particular, Jesse and Clif have continued to be generous with their time and effort as I have revised the manuscript. Others have also provided invaluable guidance, from helping me work through various ideas for chapter structures and case studies, to providing me with helpful suggestions about where to go for further research, to reading chapters and parts of chapters. These include (in alphabetical order): Kaja Cook, Becky Ellis, Michelle Mann, Robert McLain, Brenna Miller, and Ashley Wright. I also want to thank Charles Cavaliere at Oxford University Press, and the peer reviewers: Jason Dormady, Central Washington University; Tara Dixon, Northeastern University; Jason Ripper, Everett Community College; Erin O'Donnell, East Stroudsburg University of Pennsylvania; Douglas T. McGetchin, Florida Atlantic University; W. Brian Newsome, Elizabethtown College; Marko Maunula, Clayton State University; Nicola Foote, Florida Gulf Coast University; Molly A. Warsh, University of Pittsburgh; Abigail Markwyn, Carroll University; Robert A. McLain, California State University at Fullerton; Bonnie G. Smith, Rutgers University; and Amanda Izzo, Saint Louis University—all of whom offered helpful suggestions and pushed me to go that step further. Any remaining errors are my own.

I also want to thank my family, whose patience and support in this project, as in many others, is always unwavering and unstinting.

Connecting Past and Present

L et's begin with events taking place in the last few years. Here's one: in early 2019, Starbucks announced plans to replace plastic straws with recyclable polypropylene lids. "Starbucks is finally drawing a line in the sand and creating a mold for other brands to follow," stated the company's director of packaging. Some supporters see the move as a good example of a market-based solution to environmental damage. Critics warn that it's unlikely that many "green" lids will end up at recycling facilities, since the plan is only slated for stores in two of the seventy-six countries where the company operates, the United States and Canada, which recycle very few polypropylene plastics. Most people agree, though, that plastic pollution has become a problem; worldwide production of plastics in the last few generations has skyrocketed. Many plastics produced today only ever get used for just a few minutes or hours, and then are left for centuries to pollute the earth. Plastics float in enormous masses in our oceans, killing birds, fish, seals, whales, and turtles. They break down into microplastics, making their way into all kinds of organisms. Microplastics found in drinking water are even changing humans' body chemistry. Whose responsibility is it to solve this problem? What solutions are likely to be effective? We will be in a better position to answer those questions if we stop to understand the economic, cultural, political, and social forces that allowed such widespread global plastic pollution to develop in the first place.

Here's another example: on January 28, 2019 the rapper 21 Savage sang a lyric on NBC's *Late Night with Jimmy Fallon* criticizing the US government's policy of separating children from parents who had arrived at the US–Mexico border seeking asylum. A few days later, the US Immigration and Customs Enforcement (ICE) arrested 21 Savage, just a week before the Grammy Awards, for which he had been nominated for his recent collaboration with Post Malone. It turns out the Atlanta-based musician had been brought to the United States as a minor by his parents, who failed to renew his visa when it expired. During the Grammys, 21 Savage sat in an ICE detention facility. Supporters of 21 Savage applaud his bringing attention to what they consider an inhumane US immigration policy. Those who disagree with him emphasize the importance of protecting the integrity of national borders and prosecuting violations of American immigration laws. 21 Savage's case became part of a nationwide debate in the United States about the arrival of asylum seekers fleeing gang violence in El Salvador, Guatemala, and Honduras, and the US government's policy of incarcerating children and separating them from their parents. Disagreements on this issue have overlapped with discussions about asylum-seekers from the Syrian Civil War, as well as about migrants from Latin America who come to the United States to work, mostly in the agricultural and service industries, but do not get visas or overstay their visas. But questions about immigration policy and how to response to asylum-seekers are by no means limited to the United States. In the last couple of years, politicians and ordinary people have been debating similar questions about immigration driven by persecution, poverty, fear of violence, and other hardships in countries such as Lebanon, Turkey, Germany, Britain, India, Bangladesh, Colombia, Brazil, Kenya, and Ethiopia. But too often political dialogue on these issues feels like everyone's goal is to convince others that they are wrong, and treat changing one's mind as a failure rather than as a success. As with the example of plastic, if we work to understand the historical factors that led to these situations, we'll be far better poised to solve problems effectively, instead of contributing to increased polarization.

Here's a third example: a man who murdered over fifty Muslim worshippers in Christchurch, New Zealand, in March 2019 was found to have been sharing white nationalist ideas with like-minded people on Facebook and Instagram in the runup to his attack. It turns out that a man who murdered nine African Americans worshipping in a church in Charleston, South Carolina, four years earlier had also been using Facebook to exchange hateful and racist ideas with others. Certainly, social media has given people a new platform to spew hate speech, but is there really a relationship between increased racist violence and our new forms of digital communication? After the Christchurch killings, Facebook's executives decided that there was. They announced that the company would remove all white nationalist content from posts on Facebook and its subsidiary, Instagram. Supporters cheered that this massive social media company was taking responsibility to limit hate speech. Critics warned against limiting free speech online. Debate has also centered on whether private companies or governments should be responsible for regulating hate speech or protecting free speech. Meanwhile, others worry that extremists are only migrating to new venues, including to the dark web, where they can plot violence free of any oversight. At times one might feel paralyzed by the situation. We want to limit mass violence, but should we accept restrictions on our freedoms to do so? There are other important questions connected to this one. Should anyone be responsible for governing speech on social media? If so, who? And how should do they it? How else could we respond to incidents of mass violence? Often discussions on these topics are guided by people earning ad revenues for every click, offering easy-to-understand and frantically delivered messages. Fortunately, understanding the longer history of topics like censorship, racism, communication revolutions, and mass violence allows us to take a broader, more mature perspective. Rather than feeling paralyzed, studying the past allows us to make informed decisions about issues and leaves us empowered to help shape the future.

One last example. As the first volumes of this book series entered production in early 2020, a novel coronavirus, which causes the sometimes fatal respiratory illness known as COVID-19, was spreading rapidly throughout the world. First detected in Wuhan, China in late 2019, coronavirus spread to 183 countries and territories in a matter of months. By early April 2020 more than 73,000 people had died, with more than 1.3 million confirmed infections.

In response to this pandemic, national governments have taken uneven measures. South Korea aggressively tested, tracked, and treated in order to slow the spread of the disease. British Prime Minister Boris Johnson faced criticism for his government's more meager response. Johnson delayed the closure of schools, bars, restaurants, museums, and other common gathering spots, even as positive cases in the United Kingdom surpassed 1,300 in mid-March. By early April, Johnson himself landed in intensive care with COVID-19 symptoms.

While we do not yet know the long-term outcomes of the coronavirus pandemic, it has already begun to expose the degree to which the rapid circulation of goods and people throughout the world exposes us all to health threats, even if it does so unevenly. This novel coronavirus has revealed deep global inequities in access to medical care, adequate nutrition, and stable employment that make one more or less likely to contract and survive disease. It has left many societies caught up in a web of just-in-time supply chains woefully underprepared to combat the health threat. The pandemic has exposed the dangers of rapid global travel in spreading disease and highlighted humans' reliance on that same global transportation to share medical supplies and healthcare personnel. Many advocates of open borders around the world, for example, are supporting border closures to slow the spread of the disease. At least in April 2020, many politicians in the United States seem to be rapidly shifting their positions on policies related to incarceration, debt collection, healthcare, and guaranteed basic income. The pandemic has also raised important questions about the threats to public health from the intentional and unintentional spread of disinformation. In short order, coronavirus has made us all comprehend just how dependent we are on our fellow humans, for better and for worse. Coronavirus did not create the problems that it has exposed. A purely medical response to the disease will not solve those problems either. But understanding the historical origins of intertwined economic, political, and social developments that shape its spread will put all of us in a better position to address current and future problems rendered acute by disease.

It is the premise of this book series that understanding and addressing the aforementioned issues and others facing us today requires understanding their deep and global historical roots. Today's problems are not simply the outcomes of decisions yesterday—they are shaped by years, decades, and centuries of historical developments. A deep historical understanding helps us understand the present-day world in more sophisticated, mature, and reasoned ways. Humans have been interconnected with faraway places for centuries; solving the central problems facing our world means understanding those connections over time.

Too often our popular political dialogue—increasingly driven by social media, partisan politics, and short-term economic interests—ignores or discounts the complex historical dimensions of current issues and thus fails to provide useful contexts for those issues that could help citizens and leaders resolve them. Historians can help their fellow citizens make decisions by explaining the historical developments that created the world we inherited.

Rather than survey all of world history, each book in this series begins in the present with a pressing or seemingly intractable problem facing humanity (i.e., climate change, terrorism, racism, poverty). It then helps us better understand that not only is that problem not intractable, but it has historical origins. That is, it has not been a problem since time immemorial, nor is it unique to the present. Rather, problems have historical lives, have undergone changes both subtle and dramatic, and are the outcomes of human decisions and actions. The book in front of you and others in this series will help you: (1) understand the deep historical roots of a pressing and controversial issue facing the world today; (2) understand its global context; (3) interpret evidence to make reasoned, mature conclusions; (4) evaluate the arguments of others surrounding those issues; and (5) identify and utilize research skills to make independent conclusions about contemporary issues of interest to you.

The Case for the Roots of Contemporary Issues

Five central arguments shape this series' scope. First, every book explains why history matters now. Widespread consensus abounds that history helps individuals make reasonable decisions about the present and future. This is why so many governments require that their citizens study history. And yet in the United States at least, history is pretty consistently among the least popular subjects for high school and college students. Why is this? The answer is probably in part because it is required and because we give so much attention in our society to prioritizing personal and short-term interests, such that studying history seems impractical. Books in this series are explicit about how essential, practical, and empowering studying history is.

Second, all books in the series offer world history, rather than histories of "civilizations" or continents. None of these books, for instance, stops at the history of the "West." There is a good reason for this: the very idea of the "West" only emerged as an effort to imagine a fundamental civilizational distinctiveness that has never existed. The "West" developed in response to interactions between people in Europe and North America with peoples around the world. The "West" offered a politically motivated myth of a linear inheritance from Greece and Rome to modern Europe, and from modern Europe to the United States. But many facts had to be omitted (intentionally or unintentionally) to sustain that argument.

The idea of the "West" had its core in some kind of definition of Europe, and tacked on the majority-white populations in settler colonies in North America, Australia, and elsewhere. That is, the definition of the "West" is rooted in ideas about race and in global racism, which were not just products of internal developments (i.e., developments taking place exclusively within Europe and the United States), but also of the centuries-long interactions of people around the globe, including systems of colonialism and slavery. In short, these volumes recognize that humans have interacted across large spaces for centuries, and that many of the geographical terms that we use to understand the world—the West, Middle East, the Far East, Europe, America, Africa—only came to exist as products of those interactions.

Third, while all volumes in the series offer world histories, they are also different from most world histories in that they focus on the history of a specific issue. In our view, a central challenge facing a lot of world history is the magnitude of coverage required by adopting a global scope. Some solve this problem by dividing up the world into continents. That approach can be effective, but suffers from the same challenge as books that adopt civilizational paradigms like "the West." Others attempt to solve the problem by adopting global narratives that replace older civilizational ones. A global approach can help us see patterns previously overlooked, but risk erasing the complexity of human experiences and decisions in order to tell universalizing stories that can make the outcomes look inevitable. They often do not capture the extent to which even major outcomes—political revolutions, technological changes, economic transformations—are the products of decisions made by ordinary people. Neither can they capture the logical counterpoint: that those people could have made other decisions, and that ordinary people actually do transform the world every day.

The fourth argument that shapes the scope of this series relates to the interconnection between premodern and modern history. What does "modern" signify in the first place? Most understandings of the past rely on this concept, but its meaning is notoriously hard to pin down. One easy way to think about the options is to look at how historians have divided up history into premodern and modern eras in textbooks and classes.

One common dividing point is 1500. The argument here is that a set of shifts between roughly 1450 and 1550 fundamentally transformed the world so that the periods after and before this period can be understood as distinct from one another. These include global explorations, the information revolution associated with the invention of the printing press, a set of military campaigns that established the boundaries of lands ruled by Muslim and Christian princes, and the spread of Renaissance capitalism.

Another common dividing point between the modern and premodern is 1800. Critical here are the development of industrial production and transportation, democratic forms of governance, waves of anti-colonial revolutions in the Americas, novel forms of Western imperialism that came to dominate much of Africa and Asia, the intensification of scientific understandings of the world, and the spread of new secular ideologies, like nationalism. There are other dividing points that historians have used to separate history, but these two are the most common.

Regardless of which breaking point you find most convincing, there are at least two problems with this way of dividing histories along "modern" and "premodern" lines. First, these divisions are usually Eurocentric in orientation. They presuppose that "modernity" was invented in Europe, and then exported elsewhere. As a result, peoples whose histories are divided up differently or that are less marked by European norms wrongly appear "backward." The second problem with these divisions is that they are less capable of identifying continuities across these divides.

We are not arguing that distinguishing between "modern" and "premodern" is always problematic. Rather, we see advantages to framing histories *across* these divides. Histories that only cover the modern period sometimes simplify the premodern world or treat people who lived long ago as irrelevant, often missing important early legacies. Meanwhile, histories that only cover premodern periods often suffer because their relevance for understanding the present is hard to see. They sometimes ask questions of interest to only professional historians with specialized knowledge. This series seeks to correct for each of these problems by looking for premodern inheritances in the modern world.

The final argument that shapes the series is that we have a stronger understanding of developments when we study the interrelationships between large structures of power, processes of change, and individual responses to both. The books work to help you understand how history has unfolded by examining the past from these three interactive perspectives. The first is structural: how political, economic, social, and cultural power functioned at specific times and places. The second explains what forces have led to transformations from one condition to another. The third looks at how individuals have responded to both structures and changes, including how they resisted structures of power in ways that promoted change.

Historians distinguish between structure, change, and agency. Leaving out agency can make structures and changes look inevitable. Leaving out change flattens out the world, as if it were always the same (hint: always be skeptical of a sentence that begins with: "Throughout history"!). Leaving out structures celebrates human choices and autonomy, but naively ignores how broader contexts limit or shape our options. Understanding how structure, change, and agency interact allows us to create a more realistic picture of how the world works.

Doing History

When we talk to authors about writing these books, we urge that they do not need to provide all the answers to the issues that they write about, but should instead provide readers with the skills to find answers for themselves. That is, using the goals just described, this series is meant to help you think more critically about the relationship between the past and the present by developing discrete but mutually reinforcing research and analytical skills.

First, the volumes in this series will help you learn how to ask critical historical questions about contemporary issues—questions that do not beg simplistic answers but instead probe more deeply into the past, bridge seemingly disconnected geographies, and recognize the variety of human experiences. Second, you will learn how to assess, integrate, and compare the arguments of scholars who study both historical and contemporary issues. Historians do not always agree about cause and effect, the relative importance of certain contributing factors over others, or even how best to interpret a single document. This series will help you understand the importance of these debates and to find your own voice within them.

Third, you will learn how to identify, evaluate, interpret, and organize varieties of primary sources—evidence that comes from the periods you are studying—related to specific historical processes. Primary sources are the raw evidence contained in the historical record, produced at the time of an event or process either by a person or group of people directly involved or by a first-hand observer. Primary sources nearly always require historians to analyze and present their larger significance. As such, you will learn how to develop appropriate historical contexts within which to situate primary sources.

While we listed these three sets of skills in order, in fact you might begin with any one of them. For example, you may already have a historical question in mind after reading several recent news articles about a contemporary problem. That question would allow you to begin searching for appropriate debates about the historical origins of that problem or to seek out primary sources for analysis. Conversely, you might begin searching for primary sources on a topic of interest to you and then use those primary sources to frame your question. Likewise, you may start with an understanding of two opposing viewpoints about the historical origins of the problem and then conduct your own investigation into the evidence to determine which viewpoint ultimately holds up.

But only after you have developed each of these skills will you be in a position to practice a fourth critical skill: producing analytical arguments backed by historical evidence and situated within appropriate scholarly debates and historical contexts. Posing such arguments will allow you to make reasoned, mature conclusions about how history helps us all address societal problems with that same reason and maturity. We have asked authors to model and at times talk through these skills as they pertain to the issue they have contributed to the series.

Series Organization

Each volume in this series falls under one of five primary themes in history. None attempt to offer a comprehensive treatment of all facets of a theme, but instead will expose you to more specific and focused histories and questions clearly relevant to understanding the past's impact on the present.

The first theme—Humans and the Environment—investigates how we have interacted with the natural world over time. It considers how the environment shapes human life, but also how humans have impacted the environment by examining economic, social, cultural, and political developments. The second theme, Globalization, allows us to put our relationship to the natural world into a greater sense of motion. It explores the transformations that have occurred as human relationships have developed across vast distances over centuries. The third theme, the Roots of Inequality, explores the great disparities (the "haves" and "have-nots") of the world around us, along lines of race, gender, class, or other differences. This approach allows us to ask questions about the origins of inequality, and how the inequalities in the world today relate to earlier eras, including the past five hundred years of globalization.

Diverse Ways of Thinking, the fourth theme, helps us understand the past's diverse peoples on their own terms and to get a sense of how they understood one another and the world around them. It addresses the historical nature of ideologies and worldviews that people have developed to conceptualize the differences and inequalities addressed in the inequality theme. The fifth theme, the Roots of Contemporary Conflicts, explores the historical roots of conflicts rooted in diverse worldviews, environmental change, inequalities, and global interactions over time. Its goal is to illuminate the global and local factors that help explain specific conflicts. It often integrates elements of the previous four themes within a set of case studies rooted in the past but also helps explain the dramatic changes we experience and witness in the present.

Our thematic organization is meant to provide coherence and structure to a series intended to keep up with global developments in the present as historians work to provide essential contexts for making sense of those developments. Every subject facing the world today—from responding to COVID-19 to debates about the death penalty, from transgender rights to coal production, and from

the Boko Haram rebellion in Nigeria to micro-aggressions in Massachusetts—
can be better understood by considering the topic in the context of world history.

History is not a path toward easy solutions: we cannot simply copy the rec-
ommendations of Mohandas Gandhi, Sojourner Truth, Karl Marx, Ibn Rushd, or
anyone else for that matter, to solve problems today. To do so would be foolhardy.
But we can better understand the complex nature of the problems we face so that
the solutions we develop are mature, responsible, thoughtful, and informed. In
the following book, we have asked one historian with specialized knowledge and
training in this approach to guide you through this process for one specific urgent
issue facing the world.

—Jesse Spohnholz and Clif Stratton

ROOTS OF CONTEMPORARY ISSUES

GENDER RULES

At some point in the last year, you have very likely been asked to pick a pronoun for yourself. This may have happened when you were filling out a form to enroll in college. You may have done it when you were asked to specify by a teacher in a class. While a student doing the same only a few years ago probably had only two options, you may well have had three options: he/him/his; she/her/hers; or they/their/theirs. You might have thought about which ones you would choose, or you might not have given the choice much consideration at all.

In some ways this is a simple choice, one that you may have been making for your entire life—do you identify as "masculine," as "feminine," or as neither? The answer may have always been the same, or it might have changed (and might continue to change throughout your lifetime). In other ways, though—and as well see throughout the course of this book—your choice and your identification with a particular gender is enormously complex.

Gender infuses almost everything that we do and the ways that we perceive the world. For many people, gender is an intimate part of almost everything because their languages are "gender-inflected." In German, Spanish, or French, for instance, you must add an *der/die*, an *un/une*, or an *la/el* before a noun, thus gendering the noun and in the process imbuing it with hidden expectations of its characteristics. For example, in Spanish, a table (*la mesa*) is feminine, while a car (*el coche*) is masculine. English is different from these languages in that it is a "neutral gender language" in which we can add an adjective to a noun (such as a female lawyer), but the noun itself is not gendered—a table is a table, a chair is a chair, and a car is a car.

The fact that English is not a gender-inflected language does not mean that it has been without gendered assumptions. One clear example of this is the term "man" for all of humanity. Occasionally, women get incorporated into terms and titles that are specifically male-oriented. When we refer to each other using slang—"guys," "lads," and "dude" (for those of us who grew up in the 1990s), we sometimes mean this in a non–gender-specific way. Forms of adjectives that have been gendered in the past, such as "actress" or "doctoress," have been abandoned for a neutral "actor" or "doctor" that is now understood to include both men and women.[1]

---

1. For more on the implications of data bias today, see Caroline Criado Perez, *Invisible Women: Data Bias in a World Designed for Men* (New York: Abrams Press, 2019).

While gender is a deeply ingrained part of our society, it is a little tricky to define. A simple definition of gender is that it is a set of social norms assigned to individuals based on biological reproductive systems. In other words, masculinity is performed by those people with male reproductive systems, and femininity is performed by people with female reproductive systems. However, gender is *far* more complicated than that. At an individual (micro) level, gender is composed of a myriad of small actions and choices, from what clothing you wear, to where you spend your time and the kind of work that you do, to how you are perceived by members of your society.

However, you do not make your choices and act in a vacuum; you are guided by a social (macro) level, and the "norms" of gender and what society as a whole expects. In this way, the *system* of gender functions largely unseen; if you follow the norms that society expects, then you may not even think much about your gender. This is not necessarily a bad thing—norms are "normal" because most people *will* do those things; if most people don't do something, then the "norm" becomes something else. For example, until the 1960s, it was *un*common for women in the United States to wear pants. Today most women in the United States do wear pants. However, it is still very *un*common for men in this country to wear skirts (but maybe that will change in the future and it will become a norm for men as well as women).

However, gender is more than the sum of these individual actions/choices and social norms, because societies extend these choices and norms into fundamental characteristics for masculinity and femininity. We see this in a 1974 test (called the Bem test or BSRI) developed by Sandra Bem, a social psychologist, which asked subjects to classify adjectives and whether they identified with the adjectives. These included "feminine" adjectives like "warm," "tender," "childlike," and "gentle." For masculine traits, words like "forceful," "analytical," "leadership ability," and "aggressive" were the choices. People could lean toward categories of "feminine," "masculine," or "androgynous," depending on whether they identified themselves as commonly relating to these gendered traits. Gendered traits extended beyond adjectives, however, and into actions. In further tests in the 1970s and 1980s, Bem and other researchers made a number of findings. For example, those who identified strongly with their gender (masculine males and feminine females) refused to do simple tasks they associated with the other gender, such as nailing two boards together or ironing cloth napkins, even when they would have been paid to do these tasks.[2] As both the adjective and action tests reveal, gender functions largely unseen—gender roles are "naturalized," which means that people within the system accept the codes of behavior as innate, even though they are not. In other words, society as a whole views men as "naturally" doing

---

2. Martin Monto, "An Exercise in Gender: The BEM Sex Role Inventory in the Classroom," *Clinical Sociology Review* 11, no. 1 (1993): 159–174.

a given behavior because they *are that way*, and women do a different behavior because they *are that way*. If you were to ask people why, they would likely reply that this is simply the way that people/society *is*.

With that being said, most people also have some flexibility to make individual choices; systems that are too rigid tend to become brittle and fall apart. In other words, in certain circumstances, people could cross gender boundaries and perform actions or take on traits of the other gender—some women have been able to become political rulers, and men can take care of children. However, it has often been difficult for individuals to flout multiple norms, particularly for a long period of time. While there is a chance that societies may accept the individual as "eccentric," there is a larger probability that the person might be ostracized (labeled "abnormal" and treated that way). We see this in instances of cross-dressing. While in many parts of the world during the seventeenth through the nineteenth centuries it was common in the theater for men to dress as women in order to play female parts, it was rare for men to dress in women's clothing or for women to dress in men's clothing for a sustained period of time outside of the theater.[3] In order to engage in this activity over the long term, the person had to "pass" for the other gender. One famous example of this was Catalina de Erauso, who traveled from Spain to the Americas in the 1600s and lived most of the remainder of her life under different male pseudonyms.[4]

Although gender is composed of these types of macro- and micro-level choices, we need to remember that gender (like other parts of social systems) is not apolitical, and those choices are not benign. They contain a complex web of power relationships that contain value judgments—the idea that certain people should be allowed to perform certain actions, and others should not (what is "normal" and "abnormal"). This is complicated not only because of the gender norms that societies have; it's also complex because we are not simply genders but also races, classes, kinship groups, nationalities, and so on. Scholars call these overlapping identities "intersectionality"—the ways that societies ascribe various characteristics to individuals and the ways that those ascriptions shape people's behavior.

To see the complexity of gender as a system, and the ways that it functions with and alongside other types of categories (i.e., to see the power within

---

3. See Maki Isaka, *Onnagata: A Labyrinth of Gendering in Kabuki Theater* (Seattle: University of Washington Press, 2015); Harshita Mruthinti Kamath, *Impersonations: The Artifice of Brahmin Masculinity in South Indian Dance* (Berkeley: University of California Press, 2019); Kathleen B. Casey, *The Prettiest Girl on Stage Is a Man: Race and Gender Benders in American Vaudeville* (Knoxville: University of Tennessee Press, 2015); Dympna Callaghan, *Shakespeare Without Women: Representing Gender and Race on the Renaissance Stage* (London: Routledge, 2000).

4. See Michele Stepto and Gabri Stepto, *Lieutenant Nun: Memoir of a Basque Transvestite in the New World* (Boston: Beacon Press, 1997).

these systems), we need to take a slightly different focus—to find a context in which people were introduced to cultures unfamiliar to them. Just as our own assumptions and cultural norms become more visible when we encounter people who have different cultural norms, we can look at the past for moments when people encountered each other. This not only makes the characteristics of a specific gender system more visible; in these moments when two systems meet, we also see the ways that individuals have to choose whether to keep, abandon, or adapt their own norms.

Imperialism serves as a good lens for such a study. In many stages of imperialism, from initial contact to establishing new political, economic, and cultural systems, we are able to see the ways that imperial officials tried to change one or more parts of the complex system of gender (usually to suit their own purposes and interests). However, we also simultaneously see the agency of ordinary individuals who had the option to go along with the pressures imposed by imperial policies, or to resist them. This tension between the top-down pressure of colonial officials and the state, who attempted to shape the behavior of colonized people, and the bottom-up resistance of colonized people *against* this pressure, forms one of the central issues that historians look at within imperialism.

One of the reasons that these top-down and bottom-up forces have interested historians is that they encompass broader power dynamics. Getting people to do something that is in *your* best interests, but perhaps not *theirs* (and which they perhaps resist), is difficult. With imperialism this is most obviously accomplished by force, and governments have indeed taken over many different sections of land by putting military boots on the ground and creating *formal* colonies. However, getting people to do something that benefits the colonizer doesn't always occur by force. States exercise this *informal* "soft power" (thus called because it does not involve the military) through cultural influence and commercialism—persuading others that changing something (cultural norms, buying one thing instead of another, taking up a different viewpoint, etc.) is *better* than what those people were doing. To use just one example, soft power might work to convince someone that they should eat a McDonald's hamburger instead of their local cuisine. We will therefore be exploring both of these types of imperialism—formal and informal.

In our exploration of these issues, we will be focusing on four powerful empires after 1490: those of Spain, Britain, France, and the United States. I have selected these particular empires because they crossed large distances (often across large bodies of water), and the ties between metropole (the "home" of the empire) and colonies are more tenuous. This allows us to see more flexibility than in empires that were more geographically contiguous (where people are more likely to know about each other and be culturally similar). If you are interested in a good general overview of imperialism, you may want to read Heather Streets-Salter and Trevor R. Getz's *Empires and Colonies in the Modern World*, which examines some of the geographically contiguous empires, such as the Ottoman, Mughal, Ming, and Qing, in addition to the European and American empires that we will be examining.[5] While we will be focusing on European empires, throughout the volume we will be looking at the experiences and points of view of non-Europeans.

While we might not see the British, French, and Spanish empires as visibly as in the past, and US global influence is perhaps on the wane, we still see legacies of gender and imperialism all around the world.[6] One example of this is the increasing visibility of transgender and third-gender people in some parts of the world, as those people begin to more overtly resist the European gender norms imposed upon them during colonialism. Third-gender people are present in Thailand (*kathoeys*), Mexico (*muxes*), in the US Southwest (two-spirit), and in India (*hijra* or *kinner*). As European empires—with their largely binary systems of gender—spread out, however, colonial governments generally viewed these people as deviants, and outlawed nonbinary gender identification. In 2014 the India Supreme Court in India recognized a third gender, stating that "it is the right of every human being to choose their gender," a decision that impacted about two million *hijra* people in India.[7] The Supreme Court's decision was directly related to British rule in India in the nineteenth and early twentieth centuries—their 2014 decision overturned the 1871 Criminal Tribes Act, which effectively outlawed *hijras*. (It is important to note, however, that at the same time the court reinstated a British colonial law that criminalized intercourse between two members of the same gender).[8]

We also see the legacies of imperialism in the ways that many people in the United States perceive the non-Western world. One example of this is the on-going US involvement in Afghanistan. In November 2001, shortly after the September 11 attacks, First Lady Laura Bush delivered a Saturday morning radio address (the first to be delivered by a first lady rather than a president) highlighting the "brutal oppression of women" by the Taliban as one of reasons for the US war on terrorism. Nor was Laura Bush alone in linking terrorism with the Taliban and the oppression of women. The US State Department released a *Report on the Taliban's War against Women*; CNN broadcast documentaries such as *Beneath the Veil*, which exposed the Taliban's treatment of women, followed by *Unholy War*, which exposed the abuse of women and children.

While the situation in Afghanistan was incredibly complex and women's rights had declined under the Taliban, these documentaries tended to flatten the

---

5. Heather Streets-Salter and Trevor R. Getz, *Empires and Colonies in the Modern World: A Global Perspective* (Oxford: Oxford University Press, 2015).

6. While many colonies became independent outright in the middle of the twentieth century, other areas did not. For example, French Guiana is still part of France, and even though it is located in South America it is part of the European Union and uses the euro as currency.

7. "India Recognizes Transgenders As '"Third Gender"' After Supreme Court Ruling," *Huffington Post UK*, April 16, 2014. See also Zainab Salbi, "The History of India's Third Gender Movement," *HuffPost*, November 22, 2016.

8. Jake Scobey-Thal, "Third Gender: A Short History," *Foreign Policy*, June 30, 2014.

context of the situation, presenting Afghan women as victims in need of saving because they presumably couldn't save themselves. As historian Emily Rosenberg pointed out in a 2002 examination of the start of the war on terror, this type of language was far from new. She noted that saving "women and children from the grasp of barbaric, premodern men, and then to uplift them" was a common rallying cry used by European and US leaders to justify intervention in nations around the world in the late nineteenth and early twentieth centuries.[9] Wartime propaganda, such as cartoons in the 1890s that depicted Cuban women as being at the mercy of Spanish soldiers, and US propaganda posters during World War I and World War II depicting enemy soldiers as raping and killing women, focused on the danger to women abroad and potentially within the United States (if not stopped "there," the enemy could come "here"). For historians of gender in the British Empire the idea of invading a country to "save" the oppressed women was even more familiar, as it was used to justify continued occupation and cultural change in different parts of the British Empire.

As the Taliban and US officials met (and, as of 2020 continue to meet) to discuss peace talks, women's rights continue to be a point of contention in complex and historically informed ways. Similar to reform efforts aimed at non-European and non-US women, organizations that seek greater rights for Afghan women also engage with US and European lawmakers in order to further their cause. One example of this is from the Feminist Majority Foundation (FMF), founded in 1987 in the United States, although it has personnel who focus on different areas of the world. One section of the FMF's work is the "Afghan Women and Girls" group, which has several aims, including public education about the situation of women in Afghanistan.[10] As part of this, the FMF publicized an open letter written by "a coalition of Afghan women from across the country" to Speaker Nancy Pelosi, Congresswoman Ann Wagner, Ambassador Kelly Craft, Chancellor Angela Merkel of Germany, and the Prime Minister of Norway, Erna Solberg. In the letter, the Afghan women stated that they would "continue our struggle as it is a matter of life and death to us but with this letter, we want you to hear our voices too that we must matter."[11]

The fundamental difference between activists in the past and today is that rather than being headed by US or European women, many of these groups are run by Afghan women themselves, and Afghan women play a prominent role in women's rights. For example, Afghan women's rights activist Fawzia Koofi

---

9. Emily S. Rosenberg, "Rescuing Women and Children," History and September 11: A Special Issue, *Journal of American History* 89, no. 2 (September 2002): 456–465, 458.

10. "Afghan Women and Girls Campaign" Feminist Majority Foundation, https://feminist. org/our-work/afghan-women-and-girls/our-campaign/

11. "Afghan Women Ask Global Leaders to Stand by Their Side," Feminist Majority Foundation, June 19, 2020, https://feminist.org/news/afghan-women-ask-global-leaders-to-stand-by-their-side/

has served as a member of the Afghan parliament, and is the Vice President of the National Assembly. Farahnaz Forotan, a journalist whose family fled to Iran after the Taliban took over Afghanistan, has started a media campaign using the #myredline that asks Afghan women to voice the rights that they do not want to lose, such as being seen in coffee shops with friends.[12] Groups such as Afghan Women for Peace, run by the First Lady Rula (Bibi Gul) Ghani, and Time4RealPeace, seek to highlight both the condition of women to people outside of Afghanistan, and to work for increased rights *within* Afghanistan. In 2019, for example, 15,000 Afghan women from all of the provinces held a peace *jirga*, in which they created a statement about their vision for peace within Afghanistan. This marks a major shift from European and US women's rights organizations in the past, which tended to speak about women outside of the US but not with them.

As is the case with discussions about women's rights almost anywhere in the world, the question of what women in Afghanistan should do is a complex issue, however. Many Afghans—men or women—do not embrace the actions that some young women are taking, seeing it as objectionable either on its own or because it is influenced by "Western" gender roles. For example, 17-year-old high school student Hadis Lessani Delijam was cursed at by men and women for wearing makeup and Western clothes, and for walking and talking with a young man.[13]

As the case of Afghanistan demonstrates, the legacies of imperialism are still interwoven with the status of women, and of categories of gender in general. As we will see throughout this book, gender consistently undergirds how nations and people deal with each other on a global basis, including such questions as who is "civilized" and who is "barbaric," and which nations are stronger and more "manly" and which are more weaker and more "feminine." Additionally, debates remain as to just what those categories themselves mean.

Structure

In this volume we will explore the ways that gender and imperialism have intersected in five different times and geographic locations. We will begin in the sixteenth century, with Spanish contact with peoples in Central and South America, specifically the Mexica (or Aztec) peoples in Central America, the Inca in South America, and the Puebla peoples in what is today the US Southwest. During this time period Spaniards encountered people who assigned different roles to

---

12. David Zucchino and Fatima Faizi, "In Kabul's Liberating Cafes, 'Women Make the Culture Here, Not Men'" *New York Times,* May 25, 2019; Ruchi Kumar, "'Peace Where Rights Aren't Trampled': Afghan Women's Demands Ahead of the Taliban Talks" *The Guardian*, August 13, 2020.

13. Zucchino and Faizi, "In Kabul's Liberating Cafes'"

"male" and "female" people, and who had nonbinary genders (people who were neither "male" nor "female"). We will focus on religious and legal texts—the tools of formal colonial governmental control—which demonstrate not only Spanish gender norms and the ways that the Spanish government attempted to institute these norms in the Americas, but also the ways that peoples from the Aztec and Incan empires accepted, resisted, or used Spanish gender norms for their own ends.

In chapter 2, we will examine the impact of trade upon gender relations in the Atlantic trade system between Europe, West Africa, and the Caribbean during the 1700s. In this case study we will follow the goods imported and produced in England and Ireland for use in the slave trade in West Africa. In West Africa, we will look at the ways that the Atlantic slave trade itself was skewed in terms of sex (with many more men than women being sent to the Americas), and how African and European ideas of gender roles influenced the trade. We then follow slaves to sugar plantations in Jamaica, to see how plantation slavery influenced gender norms and expectations for slave and free people. In this example, we see the role that private and state-sponsored corporations played in extending formal colonies in the Caribbean.

Chapter 3 examines what scholars call "settler colonialism," in this case France in Algeria and Indochina (present-day Vietnam, Cambodia, and Laos) in the mid-1800s to early 1900s. In settler colonies such as Algeria, the imperial power (in this case, France) took over land in order to facilitate the migration of people from the "home" country, or metropole, to the colony. In the case of Indochina, the French government was less concerned about settling the land with people from France than it was about portraying colonization as "helping" Vietnamese people become "civilized." In this case study we will focus on public spaces such as the city, and private spaces such as the harem and the European home, which were critical to the assignment of gender expectations, including who could exist in what spaces and when. We'll also see the ways in which Europeans used their own gender norms to institute colonial policies, and to portray Algerian and Vietnamese people as inferior.

Even as the French were attempting to settle Algeria and "civilize" Indochina, there were also growing nationalist movements. In chapter 4, we will examine Indian and Egyptian resistance to British imperial policies that portrayed Indian and Egyptian peoples as unfit for self-rule. Here, nationalists in India and Egypt used clothing in order to communicate gender norms and nationalist identities. At times, nationalists used European-style dress to indicate "civilization" and their capacity to self-govern. At other times, however, nationalists also created or promoted forms of clothing to express their own distinct national identities. Clothing therefore communicated not only ideas about proper gender norms and roles, but also served as an easy visual identifier of political allegiance.

Our final case study, in chapter 5, examines the shift from formal colonialism to the use of imperial soft power. In the wake of anticolonial movements in the 1940s, 1950s, and 1960s that resulted in the independence of over fifty new nations, formally taking over countries (and putting military boots on the ground in order to do so) became increasingly unpopular both domestically and internationally. Instead, during this period of the Cold War the United States and Soviet Union attempted to attract (and at times coerce) foreign governments and populations to align with their respective interests. In this, both sides exercised soft power influence by financing humanitarian and cultural projects, as well as by funding militaries and engaging in covert operations. Here we turn to Europe, and the ways the United States (a former colony itself) used the motion picture genre of Westerns, with their simplistic storylines and empty location of the frontier, in order to try to project a heroic American masculinity that would bolster the idea of the United States as a leader for the world. While Westerns were very popular in the United States, Soviet Union, and Europe, the US portrayal of Native Americans and the "civilizing" of the West was not uncontested, as we will see through a comparison of West German and East German Westerns.

Taken together, these chapters reveal the ways that European imperial powers attempted to use gender in order to further their own self-interests. As we will investigate throughout this book, colonial officials and colonized people used gender in different ways—to undermine or shore up claims to political rights, to take over land and attempt to change the behavior of inhabitants, and to assert the right of world leadership. We will also see, however, that these efforts were often changed, adapted, or contested on the ground within these colonies, and that colonization and colonial rule were rarely so simple as European colonial officials imagined.

Choices and Sources

While this book does cover a lot of chronological and geographic ground, it is by no means comprehensive. Instead, the point of the book is to illustrate the ways that the relationship between gender and imperialism are relevant to understanding our culture today, though a series of compelling case studies. While we will focus on a people, place, and topic for a particular case study, you should keep in mind that there is always a world swirling beyond that example. While this volume focuses on both men and women, at times we will explore one more than the other, as fits the sources and topics. For example, you will notice that chapter 3 primarily addresses women and their behavior, and chapter 5 focuses on men. What follows are therefore a series of case studies focusing on different time periods, geographic locations, and sources in order to give you a broad overview of the topic, and to whet your appetite to explore this subject more.

My process of choosing different empires and geographic areas has meant that I selected some case studies instead of others. In chapter 1, I focused on the Spanish in the New World, but there are also very informative case studies of British and French relations with Native American peoples. In chapter 2, I examined the British role in the Atlantic triangle trade, but both the French or Portuguese also had holdings in the New World, and both were heavily engaged in the slave trade. In chapter 3, I concentrate on French colonialism in Africa and Indochina, although I could have looked at British settler colonialism in Australia, New Zealand, or South Africa. For chapter 4 there were many potential sites for nationalist movements, such as when Latin American colonies broke away from Spain in the early 1800s, or during another wave of political revolutions in the late nineteenth and early twentieth centuries. For chapter 5, I focus on Western films as a case study to understand changing gender roles during the Cold War. However, one could also study the politics of American music—particularly jazz and rock n' roll within Europe and Latin America.

In the process of writing this volume, I used a variety of primary and secondary sources. I looked in my university's library database to begin finding sources. I began by looking up my topic, using search techniques such as putting phrases in quotes, such as "Spanish empire" and "New World." Once I found a bibliographic entry that looked promising, I used several techniques to find more sources: exploring Library of Congress subject headings to see other books on that topic; searching for books and articles written by a particular author; and going to the library shelves to see what other books were shelved nearby that might relate to my topic. When I found books that were relevant to my topic I also explored their bibliographies and footnotes, which led to new (and often excellent) sources that I hadn't found yet, along with different primary sources for me to examine. In your own research you might try these methods, and don't forget to talk to your school's librarian—they are excellent resources for where and how to find information.

Ultimately, I hope that in the process of our examination of gender and imperialism, you will be able to uncover the ways that gender functions in your own life today. To use the words of noted scholar Edward Said, who was quoting a theorist named Antonio Gramsci, you should engage in a project of "'knowing oneself' as a product of the historical processes to date, which has deposited in you an infinity of traces, without leaving an inventory."[14] In this book we will explore over four hundred years of contacts between diverse and complex systems of gender, and active negotiation and choices of people to accept, adapt, or reject other options. However, you can only change the system if you *see* what the parts of the system are. Like in the film *The Matrix* (1999), you can only see the ways that your world is structured if you know that there *is* a structure. It's time to take the red pill.

---

14. Edward W. Said, *Orientalism* (New York: Pantheon Books, 1978), 25.

1

LAW AND RELIGION IN SPANISH LATIN AMERICA

On November 8, 1519, the Spanish conquistador Hernán Cortés and his group met the Aztec emperor Montezuma, in the city of Tenochtitlan. According to Cortés, the group of Spaniards, accompanied by their indigenous woman interpreter, Malintzin, were involved in an extensive ritual of welcoming in which they were greeted by the noblemen and -women of the city, as well as Montezuma and his closest lords, who gave the Spanish different valuable gifts. Cortés claimed that Montezuma gave a speech that connected the arrival of the Spanish to the Aztec understanding of dynasties, arguing that the Spanish were now the rightful rulers, and were to be obeyed. Montezuma promised to give the Spanish all of the gold that he had inherited from his grandparents and that he would supply the Spanish with everything that they needed, seeing that no harm would come to them.

However, Cortés account of Montezuma's speech also essentially parroted a document that Cortés himself was supposed to read (according to the Spanish crown)—a document called the *Requerimiento*. This was a document written in Latin in 1510 and revised in 1513, subsequently read out loud to indigenous peoples in order to provide a religious and governmental justification for their ensuing conquest.[1] The *Requerimiento* was comprised of three main sections. In the first section, the document briefly introduced indigenous peoples to the Christian God, Adam and Eve, and St. Peter. It said that the heir to these religious figures was the pope, who was working with the Christian monarchs of Castile and Aragon (Ferdinand and Isabella, and their daughter Juana). The second section stated that the peoples of the New World (the listeners) were therefore Spanish subjects. It informed them that others in the Americas had already agreed to this, and the Spanish crown had "commanded them to be treated as their subjects and vassals; and you too are held and obliged to do the same."

---

1. Roberto A. Valdeón, *Translation and the Spanish Empire in the Americas* (Amsterdam: John Benjamins Publishing Company, 2014), 45–46. There is some debate among historians about what language it was read in—the *Requerimiento* was printed in Latin, but some accounts of the ceremony did specifically mention translators.

The *Requerimiento* then instructed the listeners to deliberate about what they had heard and decide whether or not they wished to convert to Christianity and acknowledge their status as subjects of the Spanish crown.

The final section of the *Requerimiento* was both a promise and a threat—if the indigenous peoples agreed, then conquistadors reading out the document would receive them "in all love and charity, and shall leave you, your wives, and your children, and your lands, free without servitude." However, if they did *not* consent to Spanish rule, or if they attempted to delay, the Spanish crown promised to wage a type of holy war against them, making slaves of "you and your wives and your children." This was only fitting in the eyes of the Spanish, because indigenous peoples were like "vassals who do not obey, and refuse to receive their lord, and resist and contradict him." The document further insisted that the ensuing pain indigenous peoples experienced would not be the fault of the Spanish, but of indigenous peoples themselves. The *Requerimiento* ended with a statement that this was in fact a legal agreement, and that the notary who was present at the reading would give formal testimony, while the remainder of the people present served as witnesses.[2]

As historians, one thing that we need to consider in these types of documents is the historical context. Cortés's account of the meeting was in a letter to the king of Spain, Charles V. Given that Cortés's account states that Montezuma was voluntarily saying something that was so similar to the *Requerimiento* (and thus fit neatly in line with what the Spanish monarchy wanted), is his account accurate? Maybe, but maybe not. Other original accounts of the meeting are rare. For example, an account of the meeting printed in Augsburg, Germany, in 1521 or 1522 simply stated that Cortés and Montezuma had "made peace," rather than that Montezuma was bending to Cortés's wishes. However, in response to the book *Very Brief Account of the Destruction of the Indies* (1552) by Dominican friar Bartolomé de las Casas, one conquistador also wrote a letter to Charles V defending the conquistadors' actions. The conquistador stated that the Aztec lords were happy to be free from Montezuma, who was "not a legitimate lord" but a tyrant who enslaved his subjects. Indeed, the conquistador claimed that the Spanish had come with the official approval of the king and pope, and the indigenous peoples were cannibals and "filthy sodomites."[3]

2. "Requerimiento, 1510: Requirement: Pronouncement to be Read by Spanish Conquerors to Defeated Indians," National Humanities Center Resource Toolbox, National Humanities Center, 2006/2011, nationalhumanitiescenter.org/pds/.

3. A sodomite refers to someone who has anal or oral sex. Matthew Restall, *When Montezuma Met Cortés: The True Story of the Meeting that Changed History* (New York: Harper Collins, 2018), 58–9.

As this conquistador's letter hints, there was also a tendency among the Spanish to view the colonization through a gendered lens. In his letter to Charles V, Cortés did not indicate that his main translator, Malintzin, was a woman, which was somewhat unusual; most formal translators were either indigenous boys who had been kidnapped and sent to Spain to learn Spanish, or Spanish sailors who had been marooned in order to learn the local languages. Indigenous women did serve as translators, but generally in a less formal role.[4] In fact, Cortés only mentioned Malintzin by name once, referring to her more generally as his translator or "my tongue."[5] It is a different work, the *Florentine Codex*, created by Fray Bernardino de Sahagún and his Nahua workers, that highlights Malintzin's presence at the meeting between Cortés and Montezuma by visually placing her in the images of the meeting.

As the example of Cortés's meeting with Montezuma also illustrates, one of the problems with discussing the history of the 1400s and 1500s is that there are many things we simply do not know. Written records of any kind were fairly sparse, and this is magnified within an imperial context when there are complex power dynamics in play. For example, there is relatively little said about the *Requerimiento*. We assume that it was read out to groups of indigenous peoples because that's what the Spanish monarchy wanted, but beyond that, we don't know very much. Spanish conquistadors and other officials complained a lot about the *Requerimiento* as well as the ways that it was communicated to indigenous peoples. The famous Dominican friar Bartolomé de las Casas called it "absurd." According to some historians it was read to trees, sleeping villages, and from ships at sea before they approached land.[6] It is also unclear whether the *Requerimiento* was read in Latin or translated into local indigenous languages.

While there are many things we don't know about this time period and the specific events, in some ways it doesn't matter if we do not have every single detail. Indeed, whether or not the *Requerimiento* was read, heard, and understood by indigenous peoples was for practical purposes irrelevant. Reading the *Requerimiento* was an important event from the view of the Spanish crown, but from the moment the Spanish arrived they transformed the lives of indigenous peoples not only through warfare and disease, but also through the two main institutions that they used to

---

4. Alida Metcalf has a fascinating study on these go-betweens in Brazil. See Alida C. Metcalf, *Go-Betweens and the Colonization of Brazil, 1500–1600* (Austin: University of Texas Press, 2005).

5. Irma Cantú, "Malinche as Cinderellatl: Sweeping Female Agency in Search of a Global Readership," in *Colonial Itineraries of Contemporary Mexico: Literary and Cultural Inquiries*, ed. Oswald Estrada and Anna M. Nogar (Tucson: University of Arizona Press, 2014), 147–48.

6. Matthew Restall, *Seven Myths of the Spanish Conquest* (Oxford: Oxford University Press, 2003), 92–95.

justify their conquests—the Crown and the Catholic Church.[7] Both of these institutions constructed gender norms in specific ways, where men had leadership roles and society was patriarchal (although women did have some rights and powers).

For our purposes in this chapter, the *Requerimiento* will serve as a type of case study for colonization. The institutions that the Spanish government put into place in the Americas, and the laws that it implemented for subjects there, had wide-reaching consequences for both Spanish and non-Spanish peoples in the Americas. These impacted many different areas of life including where people lived, what types of work (and how much) they did, and how they interacted with other people. For example, in colonial Peru Spanish officials assumed that indigenous peoples should be moved from nomadic or dispersed agricultural areas into towns, because this would make it easier for priests to reach them for conversion to Catholicism. The Spanish answer to *where* these towns should be located was anywhere it was most beneficial to Europeans who relied on indigenous peoples as laborers.

In order to explore this topic, our sources will largely come from religious and civic texts, including inquisition records, court cases, and wills. This is not only because these records are easily accessible, but also because until relatively recently historians did not tend to study indigenous languages (instead trusting previous translations). In the case of the Incas, who did not have a written language, preconquest indigenous sources are even scarcer. This means that we are largely reliant upon Spanish sources, with (as we saw with Cortés's meeting with Montezuma) all their biases and flaws. Recent historians have responded to this problem by mining Spanish sources for information that is not necessarily about the ostensible purpose of the document. For example, while the Mexican Inquisition (the institution that prosecuted religious offenses) focused on nonindigenous peoples, the records themselves are full of information about indigenous Mexicans, and can be used to glean information about their lives. However, using these sources also can be problematic, as we will see at the end of this chapter.

Religion: The Introduction of Catholicism

Initially, the Spanish crown attempted to structure colonial rule and conversion of indigenous peoples in Peru and Mexico (see Map 1.1) through the *encomienda* system. When Spanish conquistadors, who were essentially entrepreneurs leading

---

7. It is important to note here that Spain was a "composite monarchy." After Isabella I of Castile died, her daughter with Ferdinand, Juana, became queen of Castile (although Ferdinand proclaimed himself governor). Juana had married Philip of Austria, and their son, Charles V, therefore became ruler of kingdoms across Europe that were not necessarily geographically connected. See John H. Elliott, "A Europe of Composite Monarchies," *Past & Present* 137 (November 1992): 48–71.

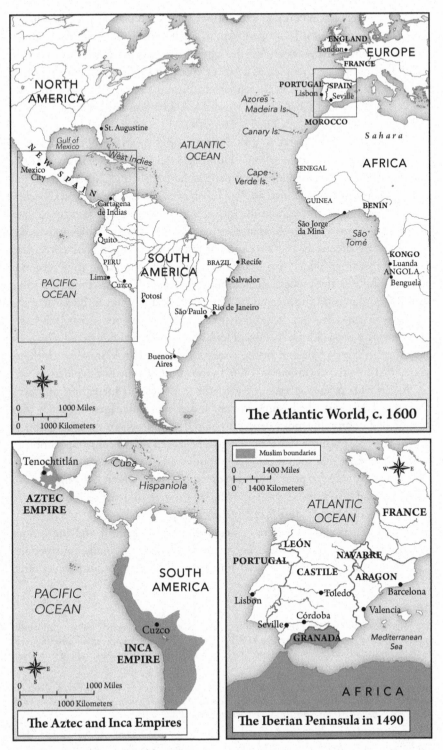

The Atlantic World, c. 1600

The Aztec and Inca Empires

The Iberian Peninsula in 1490

MAP 1.1 The Atlantic World, c. 1600

a group of independent contractors, took over lands and peoples they established a series of encomiendas. These were akin to small fiefdoms in which the Spanish monarch granted the *encomendero* the labor and goods produced by a specified number of indigenous peoples, as a way of making a profit on the investment of conquest. In exchange, the encomendero had specific responsibilities—to teach workers Spanish and Christianity, to suppress rebellion against Spain, and to maintain infrastructure.

Shortly after the arrival of Cortés, Pizarro, and their groups of conquistadors (who became encomenderos), came Dominican and Franciscan friars, who set about converting the elite indigenous people and translating Christian texts into local languages such as Nahuatl, used in much of the Aztec empire, and Quechua and Aymara, spoken throughout the Inca empire.[8] Priests were also eager to learn about indigenous cultures so that they could both address indigenous belief systems more effectively and also know if indigenous peoples were corrupting Catholic teachings (which was a large concern in the context of the Protestant Reformation). In the process, Nahua men and Spanish priests produced some of the rare glimpses into precontact Nahua life and religion in books like the *Florentine Codex*, an encyclopedia that attempted to lay out a comprehensive overview of Nahua culture. Nahua elders, writers, and artists worked alongside Fray Bernardino de Sahagún in the Franciscan College in Tlatelolco for thirty years, finalizing the document in 1576, in the midst of a smallpox epidemic.[9]

As Spanish priests spread out into the Americas in increasing numbers, they thus took with them some idea of indigenous languages, although they often relied upon indigenous people to help them. However, the translation of Christian concepts into indigenous languages proved to be a consistent problem, both in the sense that the meaning of phrases could be lost in translation (baptism translated into "to pour water on someone's head," which lacks the sense of holiness), and also because some specific terms were difficult or impossible to translate because they had no Spanish equivalent.[10]

These textual and conceptual translations reveal Spanish and indigenous assumptions about gender roles. For example, while many indigenous peoples did take up Christianity, there were limitations. First, indigenous peoples often

---

8. Indigenous peoples at the time would not have used the term "Aztec," but instead would have referred to themselves as members of their group or *altepetl*. However, because the term is commonly used today, I will be using "Aztec" for the group of Nahuatl-speaking peoples in Mexico and Central America.

9. For more information on the Florentine Codex as a document, see Jeanette Favrot Peterson and Kevin Terraciano, eds., *The Florentine Codex: An Encyclopedia of the Nahua World in Sixteenth-Century Mexico* (Austin: University of Texas Press, 2019).

10. Mark Z. Christensen, "Tales of Two Cultures: Ecclesiastical Texts and Nahua and Maya Catholicisms," *The Americas* 66, no. 3 (January 2010): 353–77, 357.

blended preconquest religious practices with Christianity. Unlike the single male Christian god, the Mayan, Nahuan, and Incan cosmologies had both male and female deities, who exhibited masculine and feminine traits. Many indigenous men and women therefore focused not only on Christ and God, but also on Mary and the saints, thus preserving the idea of both the female spiritual and the pantheon instead of single religious figures.

One example of this is the Virgin of Guadalupe. In December of 1531, the Virgin appeared to an indigenous man on the hill of Tepeyac, a suburb of Mexico City, and spoke to him in Nahua. While Spanish Catholic officials were hesitant to endorse the validity of the appearance of Mary to an indigenous man, the Virgin of Guadalupe's fame spread throughout central Mexico and by the 1600s was a symbol of pride among indigenous and *criollo* (people of Spanish ancestry born in Mexico) Mexicans. The Virgin of Guadalupe herself was not necessarily a problem for the Catholic Church—there had been cults and veneration of Mary in Europe for several hundred years. Instead, the problem was that the person who had seen the apparition of Mary was an *indigenous* man. In the 1530s, while the Spanish Catholic Church was willing for indigenous peoples to be converts, it was not necessarily ready for them to be "empowered" as being capable as recipients of divine grace.[11]

In some cases indigenous people circumvented the intentions of the priests. One such example is polygamy. Even though in indigenous societies polygamy was generally restricted to elites for practical reasons (elite men were the ones who could afford multiple wives and concubines, and used multiple marriages to cement political alliances), Sahagún complained that as soon as the priests attempted to deal with the issue by determining who was the first wife chronologically, "we found ourselves in a labyrinth of great difficulty, for they lied in saying which was the first . . . in order to marry those for whom they had greater affection." Determining who was married first also required the priests to "review and understand many idolatrous ceremonies and rituals of the time of their unbelief. And as we knew little of the language, hardly ever did we gain the insight as we have now learned it."[12] In other words, it was fairly easy for Nahua people to maintain the marital union that they wanted (the one with the most emotional connection), rather than the marriage that the priests wanted (the first chronologically).

The roles and obligations of indigenous and Spanish husband and wives seem to have many similarities. In a sermon by Sahagún in his *Manual del christiano*,

11. Asunción Lavrin, "Indian Brides of Christ: Creating New Spaces for Indigenous Women in New Spain," *Mexican Studies/Estudios Mexicanos* 15, no. 2 (Summer 1999): 225–60, 231.

12. Fray Bernardino de Sahagún, *Florentine Codex*, preliminary volume, 79. Quoted in Arthur J. O. Anderson, "Aztec Wives," in *Indian Women of Early Mexico*, ed. Susan Schroeder, Stephanie Wood, and Robert Haskett (Norman: University of Oklahoma Press, 1997), 67.

he stated that men were obligated to "seek for your wife what she requires, and you are to support your children. You will provide corn, beans, chia, chili. Such is the Word of God." A Nahua speech given by an elder, called a *huehuetlatolli*, paralleled the same advice in a story where a father tells his married son to work hard and not rest or he will be shamed by the people he lives with, particularly his wife. Other parallels between Nahua huehuetlatolli and Christian sermons about married roles included the husband taking care of his wife when she was sick or pregnant; the wife owing obedience to her husband, and the fact that he could punish her if necessary; and that a woman should care for the household, which should be her primary focus.[13]

In some cases, indigenous practices continued and the Church took a surprisingly flexible attitude toward them. Take, for example, the failure of indigenous peoples to convert to Christianity. We might expect that the Mexican or Lima Inquisitions, which arrived in the Americas in the 1570s, prosecuted and executed thousands of indigenous peoples for heresy (per the *Requerimiento*). However, indigenous peoples were generally exempt (although *mestizos*— mixed-race Spanish/indigenous peoples—could still be tried by the Inquisition), because they were considered to be legal minors. In some cases, indigenous "idolaters" were tried, but by local bishops rather than the formal Inquisition. These indigenous people were also punished in small numbers—six in Mexico (including suicides and those who died in prison), and seventeen in Oaxaca. More common were whippings, and more symbolic large-scale spectacles such as the mock burning of indigenous peoples charged with idolatry in Teiticpac in 1560.[14] However, church officials soon realized that trying and executing indigenous peoples was not the way to win converts. Instead, following a longer trajectory of the Inquisition from Spain, American inquisitions generally focused on finding "hidden" Jewish and Muslim people, prosecuting Spanish-origin peoples for offenses like blasphemy and bigamy, and searching out Protestants as part of the broader Catholic Counter-Reformation).

One example of the ways that gender, race, and religion were tied together was in accusations of witchcraft, which involved spells, potions, appeals to supernatural entities beyond Christian figures, or bargaining with the devil. The mid-1500s to mid-1600s were the time of the Spanish Inquisition as well as the peak of witchcraft trials in both Protestant and Catholic Europe, in which an estimated fifty thousand people were killed, the majority of whom were women. In the Spanish American context, three broad similarities across the accusations reveal the tangled nature of race and gender in the Americas: women who

---

13. Anderson, "Aztec Wives."

14. David Tavárez, *The Invisible War: Indigenous Devotions, Discipline, and Dissent in Colonial Mexico* (Stanford, CA: Stanford University Press, 2011), 273, 278.

were accused of witchcraft were mostly not indigenous (and thus subject to the Inquisition), although they may have learned techniques from indigenous women; they were accused of using indigenous herbs or rituals (thus crossing the line between accepted medicine and indigenous superstition); and their spells and potions focused on love and revenge (assumed to be motivations for all women, regardless of race).

As was the case with idolatry, indigenous people were not generally accused of witchcraft. However, when they were, there were some interesting gender differences. For example, in Oaxaca, indigenous women were only a small percentage of those who were accused. In Mexico, accusations were more evenly split between indigenous men and women. This regional variation might be because in indigenous communities in Oaxaca, such as the Zapotec, indigenous women did not generally lead or participate in secret rituals. Since church officials tended to be focused on collective rituals, it was indigenous men who were targeted for accusations of witchcraft. In Mexico, witchcraft accusations were more personal and tended to be used by individuals as a way to cause problems for their enemies.[15]

Race also played an important role in accusations of witchcraft. If we take the tribunals of March–August of 1650 in the area around Mexico City, we see the broad racial classifications of those accused—about 42 percent of the women were mestizo, while approximately 33 percent were women of African and *mulatto* (of mixed-race Spanish and African origin) descent, and the remaining (about 25 percent) were women of Spanish descent. These Spanish women, however, most often appear from having received substances from other, non-Spanish women.

We can see the ways that race and gender played out in the case of Isabel de Montoya, who was repeatedly tried and confined for witchcraft over the course of thirteen years (1650–1663). Raised in a matriarchal household, Montoya's father was a Spanish shoemaker, and her mother was a mestiza from Mexico City, making her eligible for prosecution by the Inquisition. Montoya's mother's family had a strong tradition of female healers (although their teachings included both Spanish and Mexican herbal lore). In her early twenties, Montoya was living in the city of Puebla de los Angeles, near Mexico City, where she made a living by making potions and spells, selling them via an Indian woman in the local market, thus crossing racial boundaries. The women who came to see her were of a variety of social statuses and were of both indigenous and Spanish ancestry, which strengthened her reach in these communities.[16]

---

15. Tavarez, *The Invisible War*, 273.

16. Amos Megged, "The Social Significance of Benevolent and Malevolent Gifts among Single Caste Women in Seventeenth-Century New Spain," *Journal of Family History* 24, no. 4 (October 1999): 420–440, 423.

The potions and spells Montoya and her fellow practitions made were deeply connected to female bodies and "feminine goals." They used female body fluids, such as menstrual blood and the caul of newborn babies, which Spanish colonists assumed to have great power, both malevolent and benevolent. The spells and potions included ones to make a man that a woman chose as a potential companion become rich. They also exchanged spells for (as the court record stated) "protection against vengeful men who wished to do away with their women or hurt them" and for seduction of a man.[17] In other words, the spells tended to be for presumed female spheres of love, financial security, and revenge.

Government: Race, Class, Gender, and the Family

Religion was not the only way that Spanish colonialism influenced indigenous life. Although the Spanish crown attempted to implement an early sort of government via the encomienda system, there were several problems that existed almost from the beginning. One was epidemic disease, which swept through the Americas in devastating waves—smallpox in the 1520s, measles in the 1530s and typhus in the 1540s, along with influenza, yellow fever, malaria, and diphtheria. With no pre-existing immunities, indigenous peoples perished in droves. It is difficult for scholars to accurately determine how much of the indigenous population died from these diseases—and scholars continue to debate the numbers—but it could be as high as 80 to 95 percent.[18] Second, although the labor tribute required of indigenous peoples in encomiendas varied (some were fairly similar to what people had been required to do under Aztec and Inca rulers), in some places labor requirements exceeded what people could physically manage. In addition to working on construction projects and transporting goods, Spanish colonists forced indigenous peoples to work in deadly conditions in silver mines such as in Potosí in Peru and Guanajuato in Mexico. Third, the Spanish crown became increasingly concerned that encomenderos aspired to become a type of aristocracy in New Spain and Peru and could potentially rise and threaten Spanish rule.

In response to the problems posed by the encomienda system, the Crown passed the New Laws in 1542 that forbade enslaving indigenous peoples, and began a shift of the encomiendas away from individual families and into royal hands via

---

17. *"Proceso y causa criminal de Isabel de Montoya, mulata ó castiza llamada La Centella, Mexico City, 1652–1661,"* Philadelphia Special Collections, University of Pennsylvania, Van Pelt Library, Ms. Lea 160 (Sp.), 2 vols., 302v folios, vol. 1, fols, 15v-40r; *"Inventario y sequestro de vienes."* Quoted in Megged, "The Social Significance," 8.

18. See Noble David Cook, *Born to Die: Disease and New World Conquest* (Cambridge: Cambridge University Press, 1998).

inheritance. In this revised legal structure, Spanish settlers were governed by one system (laws, courts, etc.) called the Republic of Spaniards (*República de Españoles*), and indigenous peoples were governed by a second, separate system, the Republic of Indians (*República de Indios*). While the laws were passed in the 1540s, encomiendos did not immediately disappear; resistance from encomienderos in Peru lasted for several decades amidst civil war, and faded out only gradually as those who held them died and were not allowed to transmit them to heirs. Encomenderos continued to file lawsuits challenging the changes into the seventeenth century.[19]

This division into Spanish and indigenous governments had wide consequences, and sparked the transition of difference from a religious designation (idolaters vs. Catholics) to a physical one (indigenous vs. non-indigenous), which took place over the next three hundred years. To understand this process, we need some background. By the late fifteenth century, Spanish Crown policies emphasized the forced conversion to Christianity of Jews and Muslims who otherwise faced expulsion from the Iberian Peninsula. Jews who converted were termed *conversos*, and Muslims who converted were termed *moriscos*. However, the Spanish crown was consistently concerned that conversos and moriscos may have not been sincere in their conversion and might still be practicing Judaism and Islam in secret. The government therefore required people to demonstrate that they had *limpieza de sangre*, or were "untainted" by non-Christian blood in order to access a variety of benefits such as practicing some professions, holding public offices, and attending university.

In the Americas, limpieza de sangre shifted from a religious context to the concept of *casta* or caste—what we might think of as race today (although people in this time period would not have had the same conception of race). One's designation in a casta was important partly because the Spanish crown separated groups by it—remember that Spanish- and African-origin people were under the jurisdiction of the Republic of Spaniards (and as we saw above were thus subject to the Inquisition), and indigenous-origin people were under the Republic of Indians. These were supposed to be completely separate—indigenous peoples had their own local governments, and were in the "care" of missionaries, while Spaniards, Africans, and mixed-race peoples who were not missionaries were forbidden from entering indigenous communities.

Even though the government in the Americas envisioned populations as separate, European, indigenous, and African people mingled together, creating a dizzying array of racial mixtures. Alongside *Españoles* or *Peninsulars*, born in

---

19. Of these, two notable laws were the *Leyes de Burgos* in 1512, which forbade *encomenderos* from punishing indigenous peoples, and required that they receive Christian teaching and pay for work (among other basic necessities); and in 1542 the *Leyes Nuevas*, which essentially disbanded the *encomienda* system, returning those land grants to the Spanish crown.

Spain, *Indios* or indigenous peoples, and Negros from Africa, there were *creoles*, of *Peninsular* descent but born in the Americas; mestizos, who were the children of *Peninsulars* and *Indios*; and mulattos, children of *Peninsulars* and *Negros*, among many other labels.[20]

Indeed, from the earliest phases of conquest, contact was gendered as men like Hernan Cortés and Francisco Pizarro had relationships (sexual and nonsexual) with indigenous women and had children by them, although these relationships tended to be transitory. In the case of Mexico, we see this in the example of an indigenous woman named Malintzin, also called *la Maliche*. Malintzin was born into a community that was on the edge of the expanding Aztec empire in Coatzacoalcos. When Malintzin was between the ages of eight and twelve, she was captured by long-distance slave traders. Slavery was part of Nahua society; the house that Malintzin grew up in probably contained women who were enslaved—who had been sold by their parents, sold themselves into slavery when they fell on difficult economic times, or who were given or traded as part of a tribute from another group. She was taken more than 150 miles along the coast to the merchant town of Xicallanco, where she was sold. Her buyers were Maya (a different linguistic group from the Nahua), who lived along the coast, and they took her to their home in Putunchan. In this household she learned two Maya dialects: Chontal and Yucatec.[21]

When Cortés's group arrived, they were the latest of several Spanish groups who had been coming to areas along the coast and attempting, unsuccessfully, to establish trade with the Putunchan people. Unlike the other Spanish, Cortés and his men weren't frightened away by the Putunchan warriors, and after several days of violent conflict, the Putunchan were forced to sue for peace. Cortés agreed so long as the Putunchans provided the Spanish food and riches.

As was common in other postconflict relationships between indigenous groups, and indigenous and Spanish groups, Putunchan leaders gave the Spanish enslaved women as part of their tribute. These enslaved women were generally auxiliary to the local social hierarchy—sisters and daughters were given as wives to marry former enemies and cement alliances, while slave women were more expendable, and it is likely that they composed the majority of women given to the Spanish. Among the twenty women given to Cortés's group was Malintzin. After the women were baptized (recall the *Requerimiento*), Cortés distributed them among the leaders of his group.[22] Malintzin was given to Alonso Hernández

---

20. For a discussion of the ways that the casta system was constantly changing, see Maria Elena Martinez, *Genealogical Fictions: Limpieza de Sangre, Religion, and Gender in Colonial Mexico* (Stanford, CA: Stanford University Press, 2008).

21. Most slaves were women. See Camilla Townsend, *Malintzin's Choices: An Indian Woman in the Conquest of Mexico* (Albuquerque: University of New Mexico Press, 2006), 19, 24–26.

22. Townsend, *Malintzin's Choices*, 36.

Puertocarrero, a prominent man from Cortés's province in Spain. As the Spanish sailed west up the coast to San Juan de Ulúa, Malintzin likely learned more about them from Jerónimo de Aguilar, a castaway sailor who spoke Yucatec Maya. When the group reached San Juan de Ulúa they disembarked and were met by representatives of Montezuma, the leader of the Tenochca, who had stationed people along the coast to watch for Spanish ships. There was a problem with communication, however, because Montezuma's representatives spoke Nahuatl and Jerónimo de Aguilar, who was called to translate, spoke only Yucatec Maya.

At this point, Malintzin made a fateful choice and stepped forward to translate. When she did so, her status almost immediately increased among both the Spanish and the indigenous people. Some Spanish began to refer to her with the honorific *Doña* in front of her name, as they would with a Spanish noblewoman. The indigenous people added an honorific "-tzine" to "Malina," one of the names that Malintzin was known by.

However, stepping forward also put her in an unstable position in relation to both the indigenous people and the Europeans. As Montezuma's messengers told him, she was "one of us people here." Yet she also spoke for the Spanish, and the indigenous people tended to conflate them. As historian Camilla Townsend explains, "when the visitors turned to Cortés and spoke directly to him, despite his lack of comprehension, they addressed him as 'Malintze' too."[23] Malintzin had stepped out of her "home,"—the traditional sphere of Nahua and Maya women—and now she was not fully Nahua, but not fully Spanish either.

Malintzin translated for Cortés as the Spanish made alliances with indigenous groups on their way to Tenochtitlan and Montezuma. In the fragment of the *Lienzo de Tlaxcalan* (an illustrated document written before 1585), we see Malintzin seated at Cortés's side as they negotiate with Xicotencatl II, who was the leader of Tlaxcala (see Figure 1.1). Gender played a role in these encounters, particularly with Montezuma, it was Malintzin who "exhorted the Indians to make peace and save their own lives." She was not alone in this; according to some accounts, Montezuma also told his people to make peace. Townsend cites a Nahuatl account in which the indigenous people chide the Spanish for making unarmed women and children suffer. The same account later states that Malintzin asked of Montezuma's successor (who was still fighting the Spanish): "Is he such a small child? He has no pity on the children and women; the old men have already perished."[24] As we see here, although Malintzin was in a particularly visible and public position, she tried to reinforce Nahua gender roles; she was advocating for the protection of the women and children, as opposed to encouraging them to pick up arms and fight the Spanish.

23. Townsend, *Malintzin's Choices*, 46, 55–56.

24. Townsend, *Malintzin's Choices*, 104–05.

FIGURE 1.1   Scene from the *Lienzo de Tlaxcala*
Source: Lienzo de Tlaxcala, fragment in the Benson Library, UT Austin. Public Domain.

After the conquest, Malintzin bore Cortés a son in 1523, whom he recognized as his own and named Martín, after his father. However, Cortés did not marry Malintzin. Instead she married one of the captains who was in his original band of conquistadors, Juan Jaramillo, in late 1524. They settled in Mexico City with their daughter, María, and lived mainly from the proceeds of Jaramillo's encomienda of Xilotepec. Martín lived in a house nearby with Cortés's relatives until he was six, when Cortés took him to Spain hoping to have him legitimized by the pope and put in the household of the king. Malintzin did not see Martín again; she died in January of 1529, when she was in her late twenties.[25]

Elite indigenous women also had relationships with Spanish men. Isabel (also called Tecuichpotzin) Montezuma the principle heir to the Aztec empire, had a similar experience to that of Malintzin.[26] After the conquest (when she was about age seventeen) she was married three times to Spanish men, starting with Alonso de Grado. Grado had been chosen for her by Cortés, and had accompanied Cortés on the conquest. Grado died after only a year of marriage, and Cortés

25. Townsend, *Malintzin's Choices*, 170–71.

26. Another example is Inés Yupanqui, who was given to Francisco Pizarro with whom she had a daughter, Francisca, who became Francisco's heir. See also Sara Guengerich, "Capac Women and the Politics of Marriage in Early Colonial Peru," *Colonial Latin American Review* 24, no. 2 (2015): 147–67.

then moved Isabel into his own household, where she became pregnant by him. Cortés then married her to another conquistador, Pedro Gallego de Andrade, although Cortés removed his daughter, named Leonor Cortés Montezuma, to the household of his cousin. In 1530 Isabel bore a second child, this time to her husband, Gallego (who died in 1530). In 1532 Isabel married for the last time, to Juan Cano de Saavedra, who had also been part of the earliest conquistador expeditions. Over the course of their twenty-year marriage Isabel and Juan had five children together, two of whom became nuns.[27]

As we see in the cases of Malintzin and Isabel Montezuma, although they both had children by Cortés neither of them married him, even though they did marry. As you could probably guess from the development of castas described earlier, Spanish officials were not generally supportive of Spanish and indigenous people marrying (even though casta categories in practice were relatively fluid during this period). Although the Spanish crown issued a royal decree in 1514 that Spanish men *could* marry indigenous women, this law was not meant to indicate equality between the Spanish and indigenous people, but rather to be sure that to institute the formal sacrament of marriage within a Church at all costs. In fact, in 1528 the Spanish crown tried to crack down on interracial relationships through a set of policies called the *vida maridable* (or "married life"), which stated that married Spanish men who were living in the Indies (the Caribbean, Central, and South America) had to return to their wives in Spain or had to arrange to bring their wives to join them in the Americas. The concern that husbands and wives should be living together was further solidified by the Catholic Church during the Council of Trent (1547–1563). The documents from these meetings included the idea that married life went beyond simple cohabitation and sex (which at least some Spanish men were already doing with indigenous women) to include maintaining a household and raising a family. For men, it also included providing for women in the form of food and other needs.[28]

Although the relationships between fathers and mixed-race children varied from individual, when Spanish men had children with indigenous women, some of them took an interest in them. This was partly because these Spanish men viewed themselves as patriarchs, and family was central to their identities (although many Spanish men did abandon children whom they had with indigenous women). These men did their best to help their fellow Spanish men honor familial obligations (such as protecting wives, concubines, and offspring), and saw themselves as being responsible to provide for their children.

---

27. Occasionally indigenous men did marry Spanish noblewomen, but this was very rare. One example was don Carlos Inca, who was the grandson of Huayna Capac, the last Inca (king), who married Doña María de Esquibel.

28. Jane E. Mangan, *Transatlantic Obligations: Creating the Bonds of Family in Conquest-era Peru and Spain* (Oxford: Oxford University Press, 2016), 71, 74

If these fathers were going to honor their patriarchal obligations, one way they did so was by removing these children from their indigenous mothers. Sometimes Spanish fathers placed mestizo children in Spanish households (usually a relative or close confidant), where the children would learn Spanish customs. This was the case with Cortés's son by Malintzin and his daughter by Isabel (Tecuichpotzin) Montezuma; Cortés placed both Martín Cortés and Leonor Cortés Montezuma in the care of his cousin by marriage, Juan Gutiérrez de Altamirano (Gutiérrez also administered Cortés's estates in New Spain). Sometimes this could mean a rise in status for the child; Cortés's son by Malintzin (Martín) went to Spain and became part of the Spanish court (although since Cortés had a legitimate son, also named Martín, by his second wife, the mestizo Martín did not become Cortés's heir).[29]

A potential avenue for mestizo daughters to be acculturated in Spanish customs was for fathers to place them in a convent. Indeed, both of Isabel Montezuma's daughters entered convents. The three convents established at Cuzco, in Peru, during the sixteenth and seventeenth centuries partly served the purpose of accepting mestizo daughters. These were designed to "'remedy' [reform] mestizas"—girls born to Spanish fathers and indigenous mothers. The convents focused on girls because Spaniards believed them to be more in danger of losing their honor, which for the Spaniards took the form of the girl's virginity. This was quite a change from indigenous societies in the Andes, which didn't make virginity central to personal honor (that Spanish men were concerned about the virginity of their daughters demonstrates the distance between Spanish and Amerindian ideas of female honor). Also important here was that the girls in convents would be removed from the potentially non-Christian influence of their mothers. Spaniards viewed women as being key to the spiritual well-being of the household. By converting the girls, they could more effectively seed Christianity in the New World (which fit with the Spanish religious rationale for colonization).[30]

In addition to religious and linguistic practices, another driving force behind the removal of mestizo children from their mother's households into Spanish women's houses or convents was that in the sixteenth and early seventeenth centuries Spanish men and women tended to tie people's cultural affiliation to external

---

29. See Donald E. Chipman, *Moctezuma's Children: Aztec Royalty under Spanish Rule, 1520–1700* (Austin: University of Texas Press, 2005). Cortés's son with Malintzin was commonly known as Martín Cortés el Mestizo, and although illegitimate was later legitimated by Pope Clement VII. Cortés's son by his second wife, Doña Juana de Zúñiga (the second Martin) was commonly known as Don Martín Cortés y Zúñiga and displaced the first Martín to become Cortés's heir.

30. Kathryn Burns, *Colonial Habits: Convents and the Spiritual Economy of Cuzco, Peru* (Durham, NC: Duke University Press, 1999), 16–17.

markers such as dress and diet.[31] In the sixteenth century, humoral theory (the idea that a person's health or disease was determined by a balance of humors) was still accepted as a medical fact, and it meant Spanish settlers thought that diet and climate had a significant impact on an individual's "constitution" and might influence physical elements such as skin color.[32] With this in mind, it would make sense that if Spanish fathers wanted children to become "Spanish," they would need to have elements of Spanish culture.

By the end of the sixteenth century the Spanish government in the Americas began to overlay race and race-based hierarchies upon indigenous kinship (although historians of Latin America continue to debate whether race as we know it today emerged in the sixteenth or late eighteenth centuries).[33] In the process, the Crown passed a series of laws that were intended to make people who were not purely Spanish both visibly and legally inferior. Mestizas were not allowed to wear the same luxurious and expensive fabrics as Spanish women, and they couldn't wear precious jewels. Mestizos were barred from some professions, such as the priesthood. Mestizo/as could also no longer inherit encomiendas from their fathers.[34] Ultimately, these laws and the presence of Spanish women meant that mixed-race children were not as desirable as they once had been to Spanish men, and the relationship between mestizas and Spanish men shifted from one of legal marriage to concubinage and extramarital affairs.

While laws became increasingly restrictive and racist, we also see that occasionally there were signs of equality, as was the case in a 1642 incident in Xochimilco, a town outside of Mexico City. Josepha de la Cruz, a Nahua, accused two of her neighbors—a Spanish man named Benito Martín and a Nahua woman named Petronila Úrsula—of stealing chickens, living together unmarried, and having many children. However, none of the witnesses called to testify corroborated her claims. A Nahua neighbor of the three testified that although Benito had regularly delivered food and bread to Petronila's home, he had done so during the day and had never stayed the night. Indeed, according to another witness Benito could not have stayed the night; he was the foreman of a bakery, and both he and the witness worked at night. A third witness, the Spanish owner of the bakery, explained that Benito gave Petronila bread to return the favor of her looking after him when he

---

31. Mangan, *Transatlantic Obligations*, 28. However, as Mangan also notes, Spanish fathers generally did not seek out children that they had with African-origin women, nor did they tend to bring them to Spain (58–59).

32. Rebecca Earle, *The Body of the Conquistador: Food, Race, and the Colonial Experience in Spanish America, 1492–1700* (Cambridge: Cambridge University Press, 2014).

33. See Martinez, *Genealogical Fictions*.

34. Karen Vieira Powers, *Women in the Crucible of Conquest: The Gendered Genesis of Spanish American Society, 1500–1600* (Albuquerque: University of New Mexico Press, 2005), 88–90.

was ill. The judge dismissed the case. For our purposes, it is important to not only note the close proximity of Spanish and Nahua peoples, but also the fact that a Nahua woman had the power to bring charges (even if unsubstantiated) against a Spanish man, and that the case made it to court.[35]

These examples show that the New Laws influenced indigenous, Spanish origin, African origin, and mixed-race men's and women's lives. While there were racial and gendered inequities within the Spanish colonial government in Mexico and Peru, people who were *not* at the top of the racial and gendered hierarchies did have *some* power to influence their lives. It also demonstrates that the neat boundaries the Spanish colonial government tried to implement between different groups of people were in fact much more flexible than it might have appeared on paper—communities of people lived along and among others.

Work: The Impact of the *Mita/Repartimiento* System

As the Crown began to dismantle the encomienda system, the Spanish government replaced it with compulsory labor drafts called *repartimiento* in Mexico and *mita* in Peru. This was a system of labor obligations that rotated— indigenous communities had to fulfill a quota of laborers for a specific period of time (usually two to four months). In exchange they would receive a minimum wage. The tasks that these people did varied and could include agriculture, infrastructure projects, or mining. However, one key feature of these tasks was that they generally focused on men, which had several impacts on gender and work for indigenous peoples.[36]

In some cases, the labor systems changed the gendered nature of some types of work. While in Central America spinning and weaving had been women's tasks, in Peru both men and women had worked to create cloth, particularly a fine cloth called *cumbi*, which was generally exchanged between Incan lords. Specially designated men and women produced this cloth full-time.[37] Early conquest era sources talk about spinning and weaving coarser fabric as a household—rather than a gendered—task. In fact, the standard unit of tribute was a set of clothing

---

35. Richard Conway, "Spaniards in the Nahua City of Xochimilco: Colonial Society and Cultural Change in Central Mexico, 1650–1725," *The Americas* 71, no. 1 (July 2014): 9–35, 27.

36. Interestingly, Spanish officials did not seriously consider having African-origin slaves take over the mining in Potosí, although African-origin slaves did mine for minerals in Portuguese Brazil. The reason seems to have been that officials thought Africans unsuited to the high-altitude conditions in the Andes. However, there were enslaved Africans laboring in the mines in Potosí alongside indigenous laborers.

37. Karen B. Grubart, *With Our Labor and Sweat: Indigenous Women and the Formation of Colonial Society in Peru, 1550–1700* (Stanford, CA: Stanford University Press, 2007), 33.

or *pieza*, which would generally require two months of weaving by the husband and wife, if they had no other tasks.[38]

When the Spanish arrived, they portrayed work among Incas as skewed the "wrong" way. From the Spanish perspective, women did most of the household production and men were lazy and did not fully support the household. One change that the Spanish therefore instituted was to draft men for the mita, and to target women—particularly single women and widows—as weavers. This was a change from the past when the obligation to provide goods to political leaders (tribute) had only applied to married couples. While official decrees from the Spanish government were often contradictory (in 1575 Viceroy Toledo had decreed that neither married women nor widows should pay tribute, leaving the status of single women in question), many women complained that they were taken advantage of and ordered to produce cloth for priests, colonial officials, and local elites.[39] In other words, the Spanish implemented policies that fit with their own gendered norms,that women were primarily producers of cloth within the home.

Not only did the *mita/repartimiento* system change the gendered nature of some tasks, it also accelerated the shift from a barter to a cash economy, as we see in the development of the mining city of Potosí. Potosí offers us a unique vantage point to see these developments because it essentially didn't exist before the Spanish conquest and their subsequent mining of silver in the mountains nearby. In Potosí, indigenous women were able to set up both formal shops and make a living selling goods on the streets. They quickly adapted to systems of credit and financial exchange, and some women (both indigenous and Spanish) had successful businesses and were in close contact with the main power brokers of the city.[40] In the area of Chucuito, which supplied workers to Potosí, women also became part of the monetary exchange system in a variety of roles.

The mita/repartimiento system also meant that sometimes men did not return to their home communities. Sometimes they died when doing the work itself or when traveling to and from the work site. They could also be waylaid by Spaniards to work on encomiendas, or stay in the cities either to escape further mita obligations or because they couldn't afford to return home. In Chucuito, outside of Potosí, there were over twice as many single women as single men in the 1560s. In their accounts to the Spanish crown, local officials instead attributed the large gender discrepancy to polygamy and concubinage, despite the fact

---

38. Grubart, *With our Labor and Sweat*, 35.

39. Bianca Premo, "From the Pockets of Women: Gendering the Mita, Migration, and Tribute in Colonial Chucuito, Peru," *The Americas* 57, no. 1 (July 2000): 63-93, 78.

40. Jane E. Mangan, *Trading Roles: Gender, Ethnicity, and the Urban Economy in Colonial Potosí* (Durham: Duke University Press, 2005).

that polygamy was generally reserved for the nobility and few people in Chucuito are likely to have have practiced it. [41]

Because men were often gone (either temporarily or permanently), a disproportionate number of houses were headed by women. In Chucuito in 1567, almost 40 percent of the adult population of women were single and widows, living in their own homes. This high percentage was before the Peruvian Viceroy Toledo arrived and increased the quota of men who had to serve in the mita.[42] As this case illustrates, despite the goals of asserting patriarchy as a civilizing force, Spanish policy tended to create matriarchal households by default instead.[43]

Patriarchy didn't disappear however, and, there were real social consequence of having men concentrated in labor camps away from their families and cities. Isabel de Montoya, whom we met earlier in the chapter when she was accused of witchcraft, serves as an example of what many women might have faced. When she was still a child, a Spaniard took her to be a servant in his mother's home. After a period of time, it was announced that he intended to marry her and two mulatta servants were given the task of training her in domestic tasks. However, at the age of fourteen, the treasurer of Mexico's mint persuaded her to become his mistress and put her in a rented house. Soon after, a sergeant major in Mexico City's local militia kidnapped her and kept her for six years as his concubine. Eventually she returned to her parent's house, but at age twenty-one, she entered into a relationship with one of the city's treasurers and became pregnant. Her parents tried to force her to marry the father of her baby, but she escaped from them. Her parents then took the child and paid one of the city's councilmen to put de Montoya in a House of Seclusion (*Casa de Recogimiento*), an institution for immoral women. While there she met Gaspar de la Peña, whom she married, although they only lived together for eight days because after repeated beatings de Montoya reported de la Peña to the city authorities. He then fled the city.[44] The houses that Montoya would create over the following years (from which she created and sold the "potions" noted in the witchcraft accusations) were a haven to lower-class women who had fled abusive partners or had been abandoned—a purpose similar to the House of Seclusion, but run by women instead.

Indeed, although it was intended by the Spanish authorities to protect them, the Magdalena House of Seclusion in Puebla was unsafe for many women. In 1628 Francisco de Trujillo (a merchant) was charged with having kidnapped

41. Bianca Premo, "From the Pockets of Women: Gendering of the Mita, Migration and Tribute in Colonial Chucuito, Peru," *The Americas* 57, no. 1 (July 2000): 63–93, 70, 72.

42. Premo, "From the Pockets of Women," 73–74.

43. Richard Boyer, *Lives of the Bigamists: Marriage, Family, and Community in Colonial Mexico* (Albuquerque: University of New Mexico Press, 1995).

44. Megged, "The Social Significance," 423–25.

a mestiza for his concubine from the casa, and installing his wife there in her place. For some women, the option to avoid being under the control of a man (with friendly or violent attentions) was to live with other women, such as Juana Bautista, who in 1648 sold the house her husband had left her and moved into a house with several other women.[45]

A final unintended consequence of the mita/repartimiento system was that it led to a lot of mobility of indigenous people, despite the Spanish authorities' intention to keep indigenous groups in separate residential areas (making it easier to control who had access to them). When men were called for service, their families occasionally went with them. For example, over two thousand of the men who reported for the mita from Chucuito in 1600 were married. The man in charge of the mita, Lope Buizeña, stated that he watched a convoy of the *mitayos* "with their wives, llamas [and] food provisions" set out on the journey to Potosí, which was over a month's walk away.[46] Indeed, a far larger percentage of people became *forasteros* (people who were not attached to a community, who had neither communal rights nor state obligations), instead of *originarios* (who were attached to indigenous communities and had both rights and state responsibilities).

Over the course of the 1600s, however, fewer men reported for the mita and fewer took their wives and families with them. Instead, mitayos expected the state to take up an increasing role in provisioning them. For example, in the 1800s, a group being sent to mines near the city of Oruro rebelled against the Spaniards along their journey, and assaulted the owners of a hacienda for not providing new livestock in exchange for a neglected llama.[47]

Nonbinary Genders: Two-Spirit Peoples

While Spanish colonization was focused on "traditional" gender norms, nontraditional gender norms also played a role. Perhaps the most famous of the those who didn't conform to traditional gender norms was Lieutenant Nun, a woman from northern Spain who made her way to the Americas dressed as a man. Over the course of twenty-one years in Central and South America she made her fortune in the military, but after killing a man during a card game she thought she was going to die and confessed that she was a woman to a priest. She was sent back to Spain, where she became a celebrity, even traveling to Rome, where Pope Urban the VIII gave her permission to continue wearing men's clothing.[48]

---

45. Megged, "The Social Significance," 423.

46. Premo, "From the Pockets of Women," 73–74.

47. Premo, "From the Pockets of Women," 77.

48. Catalina de Erauso, *Lieutenant Nun: Memoir of a Basque Transvestite in the New World*, translated by Michele Stepto and Gabriel Stepto (New York: Beacon Press, 1997).

The welcome that Lieutenant Nun received in Spain and Rome was rare, however. We see this in the Spanish reaction to the presence of a "third sex" or "third gender" (also called "in-between" or "two-spirit" people in Nahua cultures). The degree to which indigenous groups accepted these people and incorporated them into indigenous societies has been a contentious debate among historians, for three main reasons—the sources that we have, the degree that we can assume similarities across groups, and the daunting challenge of using the present to understand the past.

Our first challenge concerns the evidence. When making their arguments about the past, historians must use evidence. But what about when the sources themselves are deeply biased (as we saw with Cortés' account of the meeting with Montezuma)? That's the case here; the sources that we have generally come from Europeans, who maintained a fairly rigid binary gender system (male and female) and tended to view homosexuality as a sin. For example, when Spanish and French explorers in what is today the US Southwest encountered people who were biologically of one sex but who performed the gender roles of another they called them *berdache*, a French term for young men who were submissive in homosexual relationships. While the use of this term gives us insight into how Spanish and French men thought of the two-spirit people, it is unlikely that indigenous peoples saw two-spirit peoples in a pejorative way. Instead, scholars today refer to these people as two-spirit people, a term that several indigenous groups today have claimed for people who do not fit into European ideas of masculinity and femininity.

While it provides us with a lot of insight into Nahua culture, the *Florentine Codex* is one of these problematic sources. Indeed, historian Pete Siegal has argued that the codex reflects the conflict between Spanish ideas of homosexual behavior as sinful, and Nahua ideas in which sodomy could be viewed as part of their religion.[49] For example, Spanish priests likely misinterpreted Nahua words about two-spirit peoples. At times this was literal, in that Spanish priests translated words describing two-spirit people into Spanish words that did not have the same connotations. For example, Sahagún translated *cuiloni*, which has a complex religious meaning that isn't necessarily negative, into *sodomético paciente* ("passive sodomite"), which had a negative connotation in Spanish. Fransciscan Alonso de Molina, who produced a Nahuatl dictionary in 1571, translated *cuiloni* as *puto que padece* ("faggot who is penetrated"); using the term *puto* here carried with it the negative connotations of homosexual behavior in Spanish culture.[50]

---

49. See Pete Sigal, "Queer Nahuatl: Sahagún's Faggots and Sodomites, Lesbians and Hermaphrodites," *Ethnohistory* 54, no 1. (2007): 9–34; and Pete Sigal, ed., *Infamous Desire: Male Homosexuality in Colonial Latin America* (Chicago: University of Chicago Press, 2003).

50. Sigal, "Queer Nahuatl," 574.

Following Siegal's work, Lisa Sousa has also examined the discrepancies in translation in the *Florentine Codex*. She points to the term *patlache*, used to refer to someone who had "the attributes of an intersexual individual and has sex with women," had a penis, and "performed some aspects of gender as a male, both in terms of speech and dress." However, in his translation, Sahagún couldn't account for someone who did not fit into male or female categories, and instead translated the term as a "woman who has two sexes."[51] Sousa argues that in the image on the right in Figure 1.2, the positions of these two people indicate that they are a married couple: "The 'woman' wears the traditional hairstyle of an adult Nahua woman, and the 'man' is cropped with bangs in the European fashion of the time." However, Sousa interprets the image on the right—"an illustration showing the execution of a homosexual by burning"—as the influence of Europeans, who likely impressed upon the artists their ideas of the sinfulness of homosexual acts.[52] As we see from the work of Sousa and others, we must be cautious about taking European sources at face value.

A second point of contention focuses around the degree to which we can assume similar cultural practices across different groups. In addition to having relatively few

FIGURE 1.2 Left: the *suchioa* *(xochihua)*, "possessor of flowers"; right: punishment of the *cuiloni*, (homosexual), from the *Florentine Codex*, Book 10, folio 25v. Florence, Biblioteca Medicea Laurenziana, Med. Palat. 218–20 (courtesy of MIBACT).
Source: Florentine Codex, Book X, fol. 25v. World Digital Library. Public Domain.

---

51. Lisa Sousa, "Flowers and Speech in Discourses on Deviance in Book 10," in *The Florentine Codex*, ed. Peterson and Terraciano, 189.

52. Sousa, "Flowers and Speech," 193.

numbers of documents from this time period, we don't have documents from all places. For example, we have descriptions of two-spirit people from Spaniard Núñez de Pineda in 1673 of the Araucanian people in Chile, and French Jesuit Missionary Father Marquette (also in 1673) of the Illinois. However, there aren't many written sources indicating that two-spirit people existed broadly among indigenous peoples. Given this wide geographic range, it's tempting to draw similarities across indigenous groups, even though we don't have the textual evidence to support it. Indeed, for historian Richard Trexler, this silence about two-sprit people in documents was not because they weren't there, but rather a deliberate erasure on the part of the indigenous peoples at the time. Indigenous peoples were aware that Europeans viewed two-spirit people as abhorrent, and a society that allowed (or even celebrated) this behavior was therefore unmanly and conquerable.[53]

However, the debate about the presence of two-spirit people in different groups raises important questions about whether or not we can assume that a practice mentioned in one group was more widespread and existed (even though not mentioned) in other sources. If so, how do we mark the boundaries of where we assume that cultural practices are the same: Language families? Geographic areas? Something else? Answering these questions quickly becomes tricky. For example, in what is the US Southwest today, indigenous people speak Hopi, Zuni, Tanoan, Keresan, and Navajo. Zuni is a "language isolate," meaning that it is not related to the other languages, and Navajo is related to Athabaskan languages spoken in Canada and Alaska. Yet all these people live in the same geographic region and do share *some* (but not all) cultural practices. As you can see, these types of questions mean that we need to be careful about what we assume is true in any particular place or point of time.

The third point of contention is how much we can extend cultural practices across chronological time, as Ramon Gutiérrez's book *When Jesus Came the Corn Mothers Went Away* demonstrates. Gutiérrez examined contact between Spaniards and Pueblo cultures by focusing on gender, marriage, and sex. When the book was published in 1991, historians generally praised it as a valuable contribution to historical scholarship. However, some Pueblo people in New Mexico were severely critical of the book, as were some scholars in American studies. Their critiques, articulated by Alison Freese, included the failure of Gutiérrez to talk to living indigenous people about their own history, and his misapplication of two-spirit practices to Pueblo peoples, when those practiced had only existed among plains indigenous peoples.[54]

---

53. Richard Trexler, *Sex and Conquest: Gendered Violence, Political Order, and the European Conquest of the Americas* (Ithaca, NY: Cornell University Press, 1995).

54. Sylvia Rodríguez has an excellent and readable review of Gutiérrez, and the controversy surrounding the book. See Sylvia Rodríguez, "Review: Subaltern Historiography on the Rio Grande: On Gutiérrez's 'When Jesus Came, the Corn Mothers Went Away,'" *American Ethnologist* 21, no. 4 (1994): 892–99.

The debate about two-spirit peoples mirrors some of the issues that I raised at the beginning of this chapter with the meeting between Cortés and Montezuma: there is a lot that we simply do not know about this time period and these geographic locations. We know that some cultures had people who performed what Europeans viewed as nonbinary gender roles. We know that some of these people occupied special places in their societies, which Europeans seem to have generally not understood. Because of this, Europeans marked two-spirit people as at best odd and at worst inferior. Beyond these generalizations, though, the historical record becomes much more tangled and political, as we have seen. Although the field of LGBTQ+ history has rapidly expanded over the past fifteen years, there remains a need for evidence-based historical analysis of two-spirit people, including their similarities and differences among different indigenous groups, in North, Central, and South America. If you are interested in exploring these debates further, you should start with the books I have mentioned in the footnotes or see the Further Reading section at the end of this chapter. You can also search in your library catalog for "two-spirit" for further resources.

Conclusion

We began this chapter with the *Requerimiento*: a brief document, but one that had large impact because it set the tone for Spanish plans in the Americas. Conquest was a threefold process: a religious transformation in which indigenous people would embrace Christianity; a governmental incorporation of indigenous peoples into a European monarchy; and the exploitation of indigenous people's labor (voluntary or involuntary). These goals were neither as simple as they seemed, nor as easily implemented as the Spanish crown would have liked. When we look at gender, and the ways that the Crown compromised on certain elements such as conversion to Christianity, as well as the unintended consequences of crown policies, we see that what happened on the ground in the Americas was substantially related to individual and local conditions (perhaps even more so than official policy).

Instead of creating pure Christians, the Catholic Church in the Americas had to compromise. Spanish inquisitors focused on nonindigenous groups, and their records reveal that indigenous remedies and potions persisted. While the Crown attempted to keep groups racially separate, not only did Spanish, indigenous, and African-origin people live and work with each other, they also formed households with one another and had children together. In response to this, Spanish concepts of limpieza de sangre and purity of blood became racialized in the castas and the myriad of designations for various races. The case study of the family shows the impact of race and crown policies upon family stability. Instead of creating stable, male-headed households, the racial and economic policies tended to fracture families. The mita/repartimiento system led to a lot of mobility of indigenous people and to a shift in the gendered patterns of work in some tasks.

These changes highlight several trends that we will encounter in the coming chapters. First is the intersection of race with gender. While the Spanish crown attempted to draw distinctions between racial groups, people continued to live, work, and have sex with members of other races. This tension between what the Crown and colonial government *wanted* to happen and what *did* happen in terms of racial groups mixing will be something that we return to again. Second, capitalist production and the desire for the metropole (the colonists' home country) to make money from the extraction of goods by laborers in the colonies had wide-ranging consequences. This was particularly the case with our case study for chapter 2, in which we will examine the movement of goods and people in the transatlantic slave trade.

FURTHER READING

Grubart, Karen B. *With Our Labor and Sweat: Indigenous Women and the Formation of Colonial Society in Peru, 1550–1700*. Stanford, CA: Stanford University Press, 2007.

Guengerich, Sara Vicuña. "The Witchcraft Trials of Paula de Eguiluz, a Black Woman, in Cartagena de Indias, 1620–1636." In *Afro-Latino Voices: Narratives from the Early Modern Ibero-Atlantic World, 1550–1812*, edited by Kathryn Joy McKnight and Leo J. Garofalo, 175–93. Indianapolis: Hackett Publishing Company, 2009.

Lavrin, Asunción, ed. *Sexuality and Marriage in Colonial Latin America*. Lincoln: University of Nebraska Press, 1989.

Powers, Karen Vieira. "Andeans and Spaniards in the Contact Zone: A Gendered Collision." *American Indian Quarterly* 24, no. 4 (Autumn 2000): 511–36.

Siegal, Peter Herman. *The Flower and the Scorpion: Sexuality and Ritual in Early Nahua Culture*. Durham, NC: Duke University Press, 2011.

Sousa, Lisa. *The Woman Who Turned into a Jaguar, and Other Narratives of Native Women in the Archives of Colonial Mexico*. Stanford, CA: Stanford University Press, 2017.

2

GENDER AND COMMERCE
IN THE ATLANTIC WORLD

In 1750 Thomas Thistlewood arrived in Kingston, Jamaica, in search of a job. He was the second son of a farmer who rented land in Lincolnshire, England. While his father had been reasonably successful, Thomas's position as a second son meant that he would not inherit his father's rental land. Thomas's father died when Thomas was a boy, leaving him with a £200 inheritance when he turned twenty-one; by the time he arrived in Jamaica at twenty-nine, he had £60 of the inheritance left.[1] He had been in search of a career for a while. After failing to make a living as a farmer in his hometown, Thistlewood set out to try international trade, going to India as a supercargo (someone who was in charge of trading the cargo on the ship) for the East India Company, traveling via the Cape of Good Hope and Bahia, Brazil. Despite a modest beginning, Thistlewood was one of the European men who made a reasonable fortune in the Caribbean in the 1700s. While initially Thistlewood worked as an overseer for wealthy planters, he was eventually able to buy his own 160-acre plantation.[2]

The world that Thistlewood entered in the Americas was one of physical brutality. In the Caribbean, as was the case with many sugar plantation societies, the work was punishingly harsh. Sugar took about fourteen months from planting to maturation. Once harvested, growers had only a few days to crush the cane, and begin to refine the cane juice before it spoiled. This meant that months of potential boredom were followed by dangerous working conditions in sugar mills that operated twenty-four hours a day. Workers were sometimes crushed between grinding stones and burned to death by the sticky liquid sugar, which was difficult to wash off.

The punishments for enslaved people who disobeyed overseers or ran away were brutal, including whippings of hundreds of lashes (sometimes rubbing pepper, salt, and lime juice into the wounds), cutting off limbs, and hanging, after which the body could be mutilated

---

1. Trevor Burnard, *Mastery, Tyranny, and Desire: Thomas Thistlewood and His Slaves in the Anglo-Jamaican World* (Chapel Hill: University of North Carolina Press, 2004), 17.

2. Burnard, *Mastery, Tyranny, and Desire*, 12.

as a warning to others.[3] White overseers and plantation owners saw this violence as necessary, because in areas where there were very few whites compared to enslaved Africans, whites were deathly afraid that enslaved people would rise up and kill them. Slave revolts, though overwhelmingly unsuccessful until the Haitian revolution of the 1790s, were a reminder of the power in numbers that slaves possessed.

The sugar plantations that Thistlewood worked on were also places of sexual violence. We know this because he faithfully kept diaries of his life on Jamaica and recorded everything from the weather to his sexual conquests and his illnesses (the last two were partly connected). According to his diary, between 1751 and 1764, Thistlewood had sexual intercourse 1,774 times with two white women and 109 black women.[4] This continued a pattern of casual sexual relationships that he had established before leaving London; one of the expectations of masculinity in the eighteenth-century was that men would be engaged in sexual behavior, with voluntary or involuntary partners—their wives, prostitutes, servants, and enslaved people.

Thistlewood's experiences in Jamaica serve as a microcosm of the Atlantic economic network. While most historians tend to focus on nations or landmasses, scholars of the Atlantic world point out that the ocean itself was a type of transnational highway, where people and ideas moved regularly from port to port, country to country, and colony to colony (as Thistlewood did). Ports were crossroads for trade, gathering up goods from their local countryside, bringing in goods from other ports to be shipped or sold locally and regionally, and dispersing goods that had come from afar. Kingston was connected to British ports such as London, Bristol, and Liverpool through planters, ship captains and crews, and slave traders. It was tied to African ports such as Accra, Elmina, and Bonny through the transatlantic slave trade. It was linked to Brazil as Jamaican growers competed with Brazil to sell sugar.

In Thistlewood's experience we also see the gender and racial complexities imposed by this Atlantic economic system. Thistlewood himself was an example of some European and wealthy white men who had political and legal power over others in a way (or at least a scale) that most of them hadn't experienced before. Slavery, particularly the operations of the largest plantations, changed the nature of interpersonal relationships among masters and subordinates. As we will see later in the chapter, plantation agriculture required that white property owners stretch and change their ideas of masculinity developed in the households and manors of Europe in the sixteenth and seventeenth centuries.

---

3. Burnard, *Mastery, Tyranny, and Desire*, 13.

4. Trevor Burnard and Richard Follett, "Caribbean Slavery, British Anti-Slavery, and the Cultural Politics of Venereal Disease," *The Historical Journal* 55, no. 2 (2012): 427–451, 432.

White women were relatively rare in the Caribbean, Brazil, and coastal West Africa (although there were a few) but were implicated in the racial and gender systems of plantation slavery as well.

For African men and women, slavery in the Americas ranged from a severe to catastrophic disruption of their lives. Although the transatlantic slave trade drew from different groups in Africa that had different cultures and customs relating to gender, in the Americas these people were thrown together, sometimes with others of different ethnic, religious, and cultural groups. However, enslaved people's experience varied fairly widely. They were involved in different kinds of work, from rural fieldwork to practicing skilled trades in cities. They lived in small households and on large plantations where they were one of hundreds of enslaved people. They were part of communities that were relatively balanced in terms of gender, as well as communities that were heavily skewed male. As we will see, historians have debated how much African-origin peoples retained their culture, and how much they created anew.

In chapter 1, we examined the ways that contact between Spanish and Amerindians shaped gender norms during the sixteenth and seventeenth centuries. In this chapter, we will focus on the ways that Atlantic trade networks impacted gender norms during the seventeenth and eighteenth centuries. Europeans began their voyages in European ports and took goods to Africa (primarily the West Coast), where they exchanged the goods for enslaved people. The ships then took the enslaved people to the Americas, where they traded them for a variety of commodities, primarily sugar, rum, and tobacco, which the merchants then brought back to Europe. Although slavery was the largest (and certainly the most inhumane) aspect of this system, it is important to remember that the impact on gender roles extended beyond the transatlantic slave trade itself.

We will begin our journey through this case study as the ships themselves began, in Europe (you can trace our journey on the map 2.1). Here, we will begin to load a fictitious ship—the *Clio* (from the Greek goddess of history). In Europe the increase in manufacturing was part of a broader economic shift that some scholars have referred to as "proto-industrialization." In the seventeenth and eighteenth centuries, Europeans increasingly moved to cities and expanded trade networks both regionally and globally. The expansion of trade created by quasi-governmental entities such as the Dutch East India Company shifted commerce and urban development from the Mediterranean to Northern and Western European cities. In the wider countryside, the increase in trade (combined with other more locally specific developments) impacted gender norms, allowing men and their families to rise in wealth and status, and creating some opportunities for women as it curtailed others.

From Europe, we will move to West Africa. By the seventeenth century, the Portuguese and others were heavily engaged in the slave trade, although British and US traders would be the most substantial in the eighteenth and early nineteenth centuries. Here, European slave traders met African slave traders along the coast, and exchanged European and global goods for enslaved people.

Moving along on our journey from Africa we go to the Caribbean, where sugar plantations were the norm. On these plantations enslaved people struggled to survive and build societies amid harsh working conditions and extremely high mortality rates. The plantation system also impacted the ways that white men and women constructed masculinity and femininity over the course of the seventeenth and eighteenth centuries, with men struggling between being patriarchs and managers, and white women becoming what one historian has termed "ornamental."

Looking at the Atlantic system demonstrates that during the seventeenth and eighteenth centuries trade had as much of an impact on gender norms as did formal colonization, in which European nations took over other areas of land and established governments there, during the eighteenth and nineteenth centuries (which we will discuss in chapter 3). Although the areas in the Caribbean

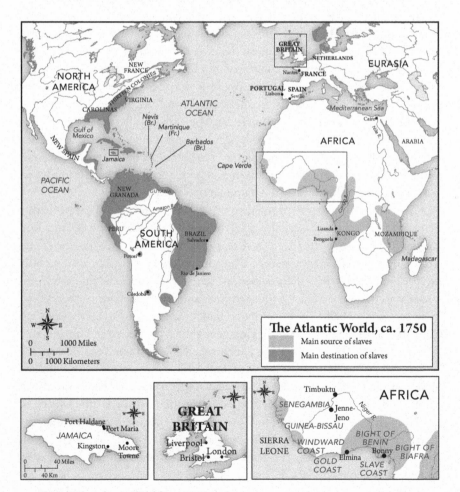

MAP 2.1 The Atlantic World, c. 1750

were formal colonies, areas in Africa were not. Instead of European states reordering society, it was the massive exchange of commodities and people in the transatlantic trade that caused rapid changes in societies, states, economies, and cultural norms.

European Manufacturing for the Slave Trade

When you think of the transatlantic slave trade, you might remember a map from your high school textbook that showed arrows going from Europe to Africa, then to the Caribbean and Americas, then returning to Europe. While this type of visualization of the trade is useful and memorable, it is overly simplistic. Because it is a map it focuses on the movement of people through geographic places, which tells us only part of the story. Instead, to see the impact of the Atlantic commercial network, we need to look at the types of goods that merchants transported from one area to another. For example, we can look at the list that historian Stanley Alpern collected from European ships manifests.[5]

Although Alpern did not specify the specific volume of goods, the most substantial item was cloth. These included Indian-made cloth, which ranged from coarse to fine cotton (India was one of the largest producers of cotton cloth in the world before 1800) and silk, as well as European-made cloth such as woolens and linen. The second most numerous good was semi processed metal, such as iron bars, copper rings and rods, lead, tin, and precious metals such as gold and silver. Merchants also traded finished metal goods, such as basins, pans, kettles, pots, and knives. By the seventeenth century, European merchants traded guns for slaves. Next in the trade volume were glass beads (the most well-known of which came from Venice), coral beads, and shells. Some African peoples also used cowrie shells (small, whitish shells which came from the Indian Ocean) as a type of currency. Ships sailing from India would use these as ballast for their ships, and then sell them to African merchants in exchange for goods and enslaved people. Alpern estimates this to be in the range of 50 billion shells.[6] Europeans also brought "vice" goods, including hard alcohol (brandy and rum), and tobacco. While a significant portion of the rum was made in the Caribbean and shipped to Africa via Europe, some Europeans imported partly refined sugar and finished making sugar and distilling alcohol in European cities. Finally, traders also exchanged small amounts of glassware, ceramics, paper, seasonings for cooking, nonmetal containers, and luxury goods such as hammocks, horsetails, flags, and canes or staffs.

---

5. Stanley B. Alpern, "What Africans Got for Their Slaves: A Master list of European Trade Goods," *History in Africa*, 22 (1995): 5–43, 6.

6. Alpern, "What Africans Got for Their Slaves," 24.

Trade in these goods could be fragile; African consumers tended to be picky about the quality and price, and could easily demand something that European traders didn't have or reject goods that weren't good quality. European merchants also competed with local craftspeople. There was a strong tradition of ironwork in Central West Africa, which produced high-quality metal goods for regional trade networks, and women in West Africa were skilled at making cotton cloth and were well-known throughout the Atlantic world for their skillful use of indigo as a dye.[7] By the time Europeans began to trade in West Africa, they therefore had to integrate themselves into these already-existing inland and coastal trade networks.[8]

For Europeans seeking to enter African trade networks, making and importing all of these goods required a substantial infrastructure and global trade networks, and it generated a lot of money. In Britain, cities like London, Bristol, and Liverpool boomed in both population and trade.[9] The flow of goods needed to trade with African slaveholders and the transport of enslaved people from Africa to the Americas, along with the corresponding boom in agriculture and mining in the Americas, created vast amounts of wealth. Merchants imported substantial amounts of the goods mentioned earlier, such as cotton calico cloth imported from India.

Manufacturers also bought goods made in English workshops from imported raw materials; for example, most of the iron used in British manufacturing during the 1700s came from Sweden and Russia.[10] The increase in trade also supported a tremendous amount of secondary economic activity: shipwrights repaired vessels; merchants stocked ships with food and other provisions; dock workers loaded and unloaded cargo; bankers and insurance companies financed

---

7. See Frederick C. Knight, *Working the Diaspora: The Impact of African Labor on the Anglo-American World, 1650–1850* (New York: New York University Press, 2010), especially chapter 4, "In an Ocean of Blue: West African Indigo Workers in the Atlantic World to 1800."

8. For ironworking, see Allan F. Roberts, Tom Joyce, Marla C. Berns, William J. Dewey, Henry J. Drewal, and Candice Goucher, *Striking Iron: The Art of African Blacksmiths* (Los Angeles: Fowler Museum at UCLA, 2019); and Candice Goucher, "Iron Sails the Seas: A Maritime History of African Diaspora Iron Technology," *Canadian Journal of Latin American and Caribbean Studies*, 38, no. 2 (July 2013); 179–196. For cotton cloth production, see Colleen E. Kriger, *Cloth in West African History* (Lanham, MD: AltaMira Press, 2006). For a general discussion of the trade networks on the Guinea coast, see Colleen E. Kriger, *Making Money: Life, Death, and Early Modern Trade on Africa's Guinea Coast* (Athens, OH: Ohio University Press, 2017).

9. The economic boom in Antwerp was slightly earlier, during the sixteenth century. Different nations would exchange goods (particularly spices from Asia) for goods, the most predominant of which was cloth.

10. This was sometimes a political issue, such as during the "calico crisis" in 1719–21, when wool merchants in England mounted an attack campaign against cotton cloth imported from India. See Chloe Wigston Smith, "'Calico Madams'; Servants, Consumption and the Calico Crisis," *Eighteenth-Century Life* 31, no. 2 (2007): 29–55.

and insured ships and cargo (most notably the enslaved people); and governments gave joint stock companies monopoly rights to trade and transport in different areas of the world and different goods (including enslaved people).

There were gendered aspects to this production and transfer of goods. On the surface, many of the people in these groups above were male, including those who produced goods that (male-led) guilds controlled.[11] European women were generally confined to unskilled, low-paying jobs (although there were instances where women ran large-scale businesses). While they may not have earned a separate wage, women were an integral part of production when goods were made within the home, even if such participation was deliberately ignored by guild leaders.

Over the course of the 1700s, production began to shift away from the home and into factories (although most industries wouldn't be mechanized until the early 1800s). In some industries, such as cloth production, women remained involved in the manufacturing process. In other industries, such as metal-smithing, household manufacturing began to be consolidated into metalworking mills, which were dominated by men. We will use these two industries as a case study to examine the ways that the increase in volume of trade goods, caused by the transatlantic trade, had upon gender.

Before the Industrial Revolution weaving cloth was laborious, with production based in individual family cottages. While cotton cloth was imported from India, textile production in Europe was mainly focused around linen (made from flax) and wool; cotton plants would not grow in the colder Northern European climate. Individual people collected these fibers (cut-down flax plants to use for linen, and sheared sheep for wool) and processed them before spinning it into thread and weaving it by hand. Families usually completed this work in their homes, although they may not have done all of the steps of the process. Within homes, people generally divided up the tasks by gender—women usually spun the fiber, and men wove it into cloth.[12]

Much of the linen produced in the British Isles during this time came from Ireland. During this time Ireland was a British colony, and the British government suppressed the wool trade there in order to boost wool production in Britain while British landlords encouraged Irish linen manufacturing. In the 1700s, while production increased exponentially (exports more than doubled), gender

---

11. Women in some places were involved in producing textiles (which would later be one of the most important shifts to factory production). See Daryl M. Hafter, ed., *European Women and Preindustrial Craft* (Bloomington: Indiana University Press, 1995).

12. Children in the household worked as well. According to Elise van Nederveen Meerkerk and Ariadne Schmidt, during the seventeenth and eighteenth centuries, 90 percent of working children in the Netherlands worked in household manufacturing, usually textiles. See Elise van Nederveen Meerkerk and Ariadne Schmidt, "Between Wage Labor and Vocation: Child Labor in Dutch Urban Industry, 1600–1800," *Journal of Social History* 41, no. 3 (2008): 717–736.

roles within the linen industry stayed more or less the same, .[13] Irish tenant farmers produced linen relatively cheaply, and the process did not require expensive machinery. Farmers often grew flax on a section of their land and food crops on another. In this process, women grew the flax and prepared it for spinning. As was the case with textiles generally, women were also the primary spinners, and Irish women gained a reputation for high-quality yarn that was much finer than what machines could do. In fact, compared to the industrialization of cotton, where mills quickly replaced household production, linen-weaving households resisted industrialization and continued household production well into the 1800s.[14]

Despite the persistence of hand-production of linen, the efficiency of producing cloth by machine meant that the gradual industrialization of textiles at the end of the eighteenth century and beginning of the nineteenth century was essentially inevitable. Industrialization changed the gendered aspect of labor in several ways, even as it preserved inequality in men's and women's jobs. As the process of production moved into factories, women became those who minded the spinning and weaving equipment, adding raw materials and removing more finished goods from the machines. Men took on the roles of fixing the equipment, a task that took more skill and was better paid. While this meant that women were consistently paid less than men who worked alongside them in the same factories, it also meant that many more young women moved away from their family households to work in textile mills. These women had more economic and social freedom than their predecessors, although many suffered from lower wages than spinners had earned under household production.

In the case of the iron industry, there was a greater shift to a centralized location of production. As in textile production, this was a type of proto-industrialization in which the methods of labor weren't yet transformed, but the volume of trade meant that workers gathered together in increasingly larger foundries. One example of this is the area between Liverpool, Bristol, and London. This area not only had access to port cities, making importing Swedish and Russian iron easier and cheaper, but also access to fuels that stoked the smithy's furnaces—wood and (in some places) local coal.

Before industrialization, most metal-smithing occurred locally. Smiths were usually attached to towns and manors, and did various jobs required by local people like shoeing horses and making tack, working on carts and carriages, and making nails—and for more skilled smiths, making locks. Metalwork was one

---

13. Mary Jo Maynes, "Gender, Labor, and Globalization in Historical Perspective: European Spinsters in the International Textile Industry, 1750–1900," *Journal of Women's History* 14, no. 4 (2004): 47–66.

14. Maxine Berg, "What Difference did Women's Work Make to the Industrial Revolution?" in *Women's Work: The English Experience, 1650–1914*, ed. Pamela Sharpe (London: Arnold, 1998), [pg range]161.

of the main occupations for men during the sixteenth and seventeenth centuries. For example, in early sixteenth-century Dudley (outside of Birmingham), 90 percent of occupations for men were in metalworking. It was also relatively well-paying; the income of metalworkers in this area during the seventeenth century was comparable to other professions, such as laborers and farmers.[15] Workshops were separate from people's houses but were generally located on the same property. Like linen-weaving, smithing was a relatively low-cost investment; as long as a man could buy iron from a trader and had the fuel to heat the metal in order to shape it, there was a lot of work that he could do in a simple smithy.

However, over the course of the eighteenth century, ironworking began to consolidate as demand increased for metal goods. We can see this in the Crowley metalworks, one of the largest in England in the eighteenth century. By the mid-1700s, Ambrose Crowley III owned foundries and factories across England, and employed two thousand men in the Midlands alone.[16] The volume of goods these men produced was immense.[17] In a 1727 inventory of a Crowley warehouse in Greenwich (down the Thames River from London), there were over 23,000 metal hoes made for sale in colonial Virginia alone. Thousands of other hoes, specifically for use on sugar plantations, were already packed for shipping.[18] (Keep these hoes in mind—we will meet up with them again in the Caribbean.)

As ironwork itself began to be consolidated into factories, new types of jobs emerged, which influenced types of masculinity. In individual production, one room of the ironmonger's home would often be designated as a warehouse or office. As workers began to be grouped together, companies developed clerking positions. There are two points to note in this development. First, these clerks were part of a growing hierarchy of work that ran parallel (or above) the trade hierarchies of guilds— "white-collar" workers, as we would call them today— instead of the "blue-collar" guildsmen in which a young man would learn a trade by moving through the system of apprentice, journeyman, and master.

This was therefore a different type of masculinity that centered on the intellect rather than a man's physical ability. For example, in a 1710 letter to his half-brother John, Ambrose Crowley asked John to "look out for some ingenious boy that can write and has served one or two or more years and the locksmith or nailing trade and has a spirit above it."[19] In other words, someone with basic

15. Marie B. Rowlands, *Masters and Men in the West Midland Metalware Trades before the Industrial Revolution* (Manchester, UK: Manchester University Press, 1975), 48.

16. Rowlands, *Masters and Men*, 80.

17. Chris Evans, "The Plantation Hoe: The Rise and Fall of an Atlantic Commodity, 1650–1850," *William and Mary Quarterly* 69, no. 1 (2012): 71–100, 84.

18. Evans, "The Plantation Hoe," 79.

19. Quoted in Rowlands, *Masters and Men*, 86.

skills, but who aspired to a higher place in the emerging work hierarchy. Second, these clerkships were part of the gradual breakdown of male heads of households as paternal "masters," who had been in charge of not only the work of apprentice and journeymen dependents, but their moral upbringing as well.[20]

Impacts of the Atlantic Slave Trade in Africa

Our imaginary ship *Clio* is now full of goods that have been shipped through British ports and produced within the British Isles. We now travel 3,000 to 9,000 miles south, along the West Coast of Africa (see Map 2.1). Europeans and Africans were in contact with each other along the northwest coast of Africa starting in the 1400s (before even Columbus "discovered" the Americas), in a trade network that was geared around specific commodities. We can see this in the names that Europeans used for sections of the coastline: the Gold Coast, the Ivory Coast, and the Slave Coast. The Portuguese dominated trade along the West Coast of Africa from the 1400s to the 1600s, establishing forts and trading posts at places like Cape Verde (a series of islands located off the coast of what is today Senegal) and Elmina (in southern Ghana). By the 1600s Dutch, British, Spanish, and French traders competed for the goods coming from the interior of Africa, and by the 1700s, when the demand for labor in the mines and plantations of the Americas began to grow, the trade in slaves began to displace goods. While the trade of earlier commodities such as gold and ivory had not greatly disturbed African gender roles, the sheer volume of the slave trade, and the fact that this was a trade in people rather than commodities, shaped—and was shaped by—African and European assumptions of gender.

One way that gender and culture interacted on the coast was through hybrid African–European societies. Europeans were not numerically or militarily strong enough to take over sections of the African coast; in fact, their power didn't often extend much beyond their own trading fort. This meant they had to constantly negotiate with the local African rulers for basic necessities (even sometimes food and water) and for the ability to trade.

These coastal societies tended to be composed of European male slave traders and African or Euro-African women. Slave traders tended to not bring European women with them, and African wives were a tremendous asset for negotiating with local groups. Following the practice initiated by the Portuguese in Cape Verde British, French, and Dutch men commonly formed sexual and

---

20. This process happened a little bit later in the United States, but there are two excellent works on it: Karen Halttunen, *Confidence Men and Painted Women: A Study of Middle-Class Culture in America, 1830–1870* (New Haven, CT: Yale University Press, 1982), and Patricia Cline Cohen, *The Murder of Helen Jewett: The Life and Death of a Prostitute in Nineteenth-Century New York* (New York: Knopf, 1998).

marital alliances with African women along the West African coast in the 1700s. These women gave Europeans access to resources within their communities. Euro-African communities were hybrid, and people used a mixture of local and European goods, likely lived in European-style houses, and tended to practice Christianity; Euro-Africans could live with a foot in both European and African cultures.[21] Euro-African children often served as intermediaries between African and European societies, bringing trade goods to European towns and forts.

While Euro-African children were a cultural mixture, their mother's culture was generally more important to their daily lives because it governed their economic and social opportunities. European men frequently died or returned to Europe, leaving Euro-African children behind. One of the main things that determined the economic prospects of Euro-African children was whether they were boys or girls, and whether their mother's society was matrilineal or patrilineal. We see these differences in the Mandinka peoples along the Gambia River, and Wolof and Serer peoples in Senegambia, versus the Guinea-Bissau region. While women in Guinea-Bissau could become traders in their own right and even establish trading communities, Mandinka, Wolof, and Serer women served as intermediaries between groups of men. This was due to two factors: social stratification (in which societies were arranged in a hierarchy) versus acephalous societies (in which society was more egalitarian and didn't have a formal head); and whether or not groups were patrilineal or matrilineal. These qualities generally went together—stratified societies tended to be patriarchal, and acephalous societies tended to be matrilineal.[22]

One example of a woman serving as an independent trader was Mãe Aurélia Correia, a woman who lived in Guinea-Bissau. Correia was a *nhara*, or a wealthy and influential woman. In his case study of her life, George Brooks states that because of her Portuguese names and the lack of information on her parents and relatives (the only other relative who is in the documents is her sister Mãe Julia), it is likely that Correia had been captured on a slave raid as a child and was raised on Orango island (off the coast of Guinea-Bissau). She was married to an Italian-Portuguese army officer from Cape Verde, Caetano Nozolini. Nozolini was able to use his status as an army officer to his advantage, positioning himself as a trader between the Portuguese forts and local African populations (given the very low pay of most European military officials in West Africa, this was one of the only ways for them to make money). Over the course of approximately fifteen years, Correia and Nozolini established themselves as the foremost traders of European

21. Pernille Ipsen, *Daughters of the Trade: Atlantic Slavers and Interracial Marriage on the Gold Coast* (Philadelphia: University of Pennsylvania Press, 2015), 11.

22. George E. Brooks, "A Nara of the Guinea-Bissau Region-Mãe Aurélia Correia," in *Women and Slavery in Africa*, ed. Clare C. Robertson and Martin A. Klein (Portsmouth, NH: Heinemann, 1997), 295–319.

goods and enslaved people on the Bissagos archipelago, and they also set up plantations on the island of Bolama, where they used enslaved people to grow crops for export.[23]

Slave traders on the West Coast of Africa both small-scale traders such as Correia and Nozolini, and large-scale traders such as kings and rulers, drew millions of people (usually their enemies) from the coast and interior regions of Africa. However, the slave trade did not draw men and women equally; men were overrepresented among enslaved Africans in comparison to women. While the lack of good written records has caused historians to debate the specific numbers of males and females, even when we account for age (separating boys from men and girls from women), men were still the largest proportion of enslaved people.[24]

Historians disagree about *why* there was such a gender disparity. Was it an issue of supply, driven by Africans who supplied many more men than women, with the result that European traders had to take what was available? Or was it an issue of demand, because Euro-American planters wanted to purchase men for the hard labor that the enslaved people were going to do in the Americas? This is a complex issue for several reasons. First, one of the problems for historians is that enslaved Africans did not produce documents themselves. Many did not use a written language, and once they got to the Americas (if they survived the Middle Passage), slaveowners generally did not teach them how to write (if the owners themselves even knew how). In some areas even reading was forbidden.[25]

While we do have some accounts of enslaved people who had been freed, called "captivity narratives" or "slave narratives" (many of which were used by the abolitionist movement both in the United States and Europe), our largest cache of documents comes from slave traders: cargo manifests, lists of enslaved people, and beginning in the 1800s, lists of people from ships that were captured and the people who were emancipated. Most of the data in these records provides little information about the people themselves, generally only listing a single name, sex, approximate age, height, and identifying features. .[26] Starting in the 1990s, historians have created a database called the Transatlantic Slave Trade

---

23. Brooks, "A Nara of the Guinea-Bissau Region."

24. See, for example, David Eltis and Stanley L. Engerman, "Was the Slave Trade Dominated by Men?," *Journal of Interdisciplinary History* 23, no. 2 (1992): 237–257.

25. The 1740 South Carolina Negro Act, put in place in the wake of the Stono Rebellion, forbade slaves from reading. See Birgit Brander Rasmussen, "'Attended with Great Inconveniences': Slave Literacy and the 1740 South Carolina Negro Act," *PLMA* 125, no. 1 (January 2010): 201–203. However, as Antonio Bly argues, there were increasing rates of literacy, at least among some groups of slaves in the British North American colonies. See Antonio T. Bly, "'Pretends He Can Read': Runaways and Literacy in Colonial America, 1730–1776," *Early American Studies* 6, no. 2 (Fall 2008): 261–294.

26. Paul E. Lovejoy provides a good overview of these debates from the vantage point of 1982. See Lovejoy, "The Volume of the Atlantic Slave Trade: A Synthesis," *Journal of African History* 23, no. 4 (1982): 473–501.

Database (slavevoyages.org), which has allowed them to analyze the data in a much more systemic way.

While some of these records reveal tantalizing glimpses of individual lives and motivations, these documents primarily allow us to make large-scale conclusions about the slave trade—while we can see that there *was* a gender imbalance, it is difficult to determine *why* that imbalance existed. However, we can also look for who had the most power—supply or demand—within the trade. In voluntary trading situations (as opposed to simply taking something by force), both of these sides do have some degree of power to accept the terms of the other side. Some historians have argued that the demand side drove the interactions. Other historians emphasize the African supply side—that African traders had the power to sell whomever they wanted, and the Europeans had to (more or less) take what was offered.[27]

We can consider the gender norms of some of West African cultures to help resolve the issue of supply or demand. Let's take the example of the sale of enslaved people. As Alpern's list illustrates, one of the commodities Europeans exchanged for enslaved people were cowrie shells, which some West African groups used as currency. In other words, selling enslaved people brought cash. However, in many West African societies' wealth was largely determined not by cash, but by the number of people whose labor one could exploit. In contrast to Europe, where wealth was generally tied to land ownership, in many sub-Saharan African societies land wasn't owned by individuals. Instead, wealth was determined by the number of people who could produce goods for consumption or sale, and women were particularly good at making a profit through farming. Here we have an economic conundrum for slave sellers: keep people who can add to one's wealth in some way over a period of time, or sell them for immediate profit.

Part of the calculation of whether to sell or keep a slave also likely had to do with the price that one could get for selling them, and the different slave markets operating in Africa—the West Coast transatlantic market, the trans-Saharan market (ending in the Eastern Mediterranean), and the East Coast trans-Indian ocean market. Enslaved people brought different prices in each of these markets. For sellers, choosing *who* to sell was a strategic calculation, and there is some evidence that women brought higher prices in the non-Atlantic markets. More women may also have been kept and not sold on because they could serve a number of different functions—from having children (who could potentially be enslaved), to being incorporated into existing kin networks as concubines, to producing goods to supply armies, to marrying slave men.[28] As Paul E. Lovejoy and

27. Richard B. Sheridan, *Sugar and Slavery: An Economic History of the British West Indies* (Baltimore: Johns Hopkins University Press, 1974).

28. E. Frances White, "Women in West and West-Central Africa," in *Women in Sub-Saharan Africa: Restoring Women to History*, ed. Iris Berger and E. Francis White (Bloomington: Indiana University Press, 1999), 63–130, 67–8.

David Richardson point out, prices for women were higher away from the West Coast. Lovejoy estimated that of the "75,000 to 124,000 slaves [who] were exported south from the Central Sudan to the Atlantic Coast for export to the Americas between 1805 and 1850, approximately 95 percent . . . were prime males." At the same time, the trans-Saharan trade "may have amounted to 150,000–290,000 slaves, and it seems reasonable to assume that there were about two females for every male in this trade."[29] It therefore made financial sense for sellers to move men to the West Coast, where they would get higher prices, and either keep women or sell them in the trans-Saharan trade.

Along with price, a seller's decisions could also depend on what the men did for a living, as well as their varied gender roles within their own societies. One potential reason to keep male warriors was that if loyal, they could prove to be a powerful army, as was the case in the Sudanese empire. However, male warriors who were not loyal to their new masters were a serious liability because they could successfully revolt.[30] Slave sellers therefore tended to sell the male warriors into the transatlantic slave trade. For example, in the 1800s, a sample of ships that had been boarded by British who were trying to stop the slave trade, "war captives accounted for 34 percent, the largest single category." After the end of the slave trade, war prisoners were often killed.[31] If men weren't warriors, however, their labor could be useful for increasing the wealth of the leader. In the case of the Kongo and Ndongo, enslaved people were located around the capital cities and provided a concentration of people that spurred economic growth and the centralization of those states.[32]

For African slave owners, purchasing enslaved women had several advantages. One was that they could be used to produce goods for sale, such as cloth. In Warri (in what is today Nigeria), the Italian Bonaventura da Firenze remarked in 1656 "that the ruler had a substantial harem of wives who produced cloth for sale." The King of Whydah (in what is today Benin) had a harem of supposedly over a thousand wives who produced cloth for export.[33] In Oyo, in Yorubaland (what is today primarily Nigeria), the king's wives (most of whom were enslaved) made cloth, salt, and natron (a type of combination soda ash/salt). Women in Yoruba

29. Paul E. Lovejoy and David Richardson, "Competing Markets for Male and Female Slaves: Prices in the Interior of West Africa, 1780–1850," *International Journal of African Historical Studies* 28, no. 2 (1995): 261–293, 269.

30. This isn't to say that there weren't female warriors in come societies, such as the Dahomey, in which women acted as a type of extra military force. Women also served in some societies as rulers, such as Njinga, who ruled in the Kongo.

31. G. Ugo Nwokeji, "African Conceptions of Gender and the Slave Traffic," *William and Mary* Quarterly 58, no. 1 (2001): 47–68, 61-2.

32. Thornton, *Africa and Africans*, 93–4.

33. Thornton, *Africa and Africans*, 86.

society participated in agricultural production in addition to weaving and making salt.[34] In many cases, women's roles in agriculture were vital to feeding the local population. Along the coast of the Bight of Biafra, men were essentially responsible for clearing land, tilling, building, and planting and harvesting yams (growing yams was done exclusively by men and was associated with masculinity). Women planted the rest of the vegetables and other crops.[35] Once the land was cleared, women's work was therefore of primary importance to food supply. Some West African societies could also more easily absorb a surplus of women. In Angola, even though there were almost double the number of women as men, the extra women were incorporated into polygynous relationships.[36]

Women who were enslaved may also have been more valuable because in communities where kinship obligations were important, slave women were without kin. This was particularly attractive to men in matrilineal societies, whose children with free women would be of the woman's lineage. If a man wanted to have his own lineage, he needed children from a woman whose kinship ties weren't recognized—in other words, one who was enslaved. For example, within Kongo society, kinship was the primary way social groups were organized. Women had two categories: those who were able to bear children were confined to a wife role, which involved "producing children for their husbands' lineages and laboring in their husbands' fields and compounds." Once a woman passed childbearing years, they were able "to assume the role of sister, helping to advise on the affairs of their lineage and commanding the services of daughters-in-law."[37] Free Bakongo women could make this transition and had additional rights, including the power to divorce their husbands. Slave women did not have this ability. Because slave women did not have a lineage of their own, they were confined to wife's roles for the duration of their lives or period of enslavement (in African slavery generally, people might or might not be slaves for their entire lives. Instead, they might only be enslaved for a period of time for a specific reason, such as to pay off a debt).

As this cultural context makes clear, there is compelling evidence that the gender imbalance in the slave trade was at least partly caused by the supply of slaves within Africa. If enslaved women were more useful to local people, or could be sold for more money in non-Atlantic slave trading markets, it makes sense that African slave traders would choose these instead of selling them in West Africa. As we will see in the next section, however, we need to consider the ways that the

---

34. E. Frances White, "Women in West and West-Central Africa," 68–9.

35. Nwokeji, "African Conceptions of Gender," 56.

36. John Thornton, "Sexual Demography: The Impact of the Slave Trade on Family Structure," in *Women and Slavery in Africa*, ed. Robertson and Klein: 39–48.

37. Susan Herlin Broadhead, "Slave Wives, Free Sisters: Bakongo Women and Slavery c. 1700–1850," in *Women and Slavery in Africa*, ed. Robertson and Klein, 160–184, 161.

European slave buyers in the Caribbean also shaped the gender imbalance in the transatlantic slave trade.

The British Caribbean: Jamaica

Returning back to our imaginary ship *Clio*, with the cargo hold now full of enslaved people from West Africa, we sail through the brutal Middle Passage and arrive at the Caribbean. Here, slavery reinforced some gender norms and changed or obliterated others for both enslaved and European people. As we saw earlier, men composed the largest group of African enslaved people sent to the Americas. Once they arrived in the Americas, however, they had widely different experiences, depending on where they ended up and what they did there. As I noted in the introduction to this chapter, enslaved people performed a variety of tasks in diverse situations. Slave men and women might live in a city and essentially practice a profession for hire; they might live on a small farm, where they were the only slave and performed a variety of tasks; or they might live on a large plantation with hundreds of other enslaved people, working as part of a "gang" agricultural system. While there was some variety, most enslaved people worked in agriculture, where the type of crop largely determined a slave's lifestyle and lifespan. The dominant industry in the Caribbean and Brazil (where most enslaved people were sent) was sugar. This shaped all aspects of white and black men and women's lives, from the numbers of men and women in the islands to the ways that different groups of people perceived gender roles. In order to tease out the specific aspects of the intersections of race, class, and gender, we will examine the British Caribbean islands, specifically Jamaica.

One of the aspects of life for everyone in Jamaica and Nevis was the substantial death rate—both for Europeans and enslaved people. For Europeans, this was usually the result of diseases like malaria and yellow fever.[38] While initial mortality rates in other British settlements that also had high tropical disease rates —such as in Virginia—were extremely high, they declined over time.[39] In Jamaica, high British mortality rates persisted, which shaped gender norms. At times, death rates were so high that the white population couldn't reproduce itself—men and women essentially didn't stay alive for long enough after marriage in order to have children. And if they did have children, chances were that those children would die before they were able to have children.

---

38. Trevor Burnard, "A Failed Settler Society: Marriage and Demographic Failure in Early Jamaica," *Journal of Social History* 28, no. 1 (1994): 63–82, 68.

39. Darrett B. Rutman and Anita H. Rutman, "'Now-Wives and Sons-in-Law': Parental Death in a Seventeenth-Century Virginia County," in *The Chesapeake in the Seventeenth Century: Essays on Anglo-American Society*, ed. Thad W. Tate and David L. Ammerman (New York: Norton, 1979): 153–182.

For our purposes, this high European mortality rate is important for two reasons. First, it led to a fairly rapid consolidation of plantations. Between 1666 and 1704, the average length of marriages fell from nine and a half years to four years and nine months.[40] This meant that there were a lot of widows and widowers who had inherited estates. Most of them remarried, only to encounter the same type of mortality rates. However, gender played a role here. Over time, the age difference between white brides and grooms increased—grooms got older and brides got younger. This meant that women were more likely to survive in the marriage, and they spent a longer time in widowhood than men did as widowers. However, this remarriage rate was nuanced by social status; wealthy widows married easily and more quickly than poor widows. Consolidation also meant that it was difficult for younger and poorer white men to become landowners on the islands, as we'll see.

Plantation slave societies also influenced the racial, class, and gendered norms of Europeans. White women were deeply imbedded in the racial and social hierarchies of slavery. From the time they were born, white women were taught by their parents and other whites that they were superior to African-origin people, and that enslaved people were property instead of human beings. Many elite white women owned enslaved people and oversaw their work on plantations, including punishment both within and outside of the household. White women were also involved in the slave markets. As a recent scholar of the topic in the Antebellum South has put it, "they were her property."[41]

However, European women were also generally subject to British gender norms that saw white women as being incapable of having the same level of authority as white men. For example, in the case of a supposed slave uprising in Nevis in 1725, the two enslaved men who were executed were owned by wealthy widows. A third man, named Frank, was the slave of Sir William Stapleton. Stapleton and his plantation manager sheltered Frank, even bringing him to England to wait out the controversy over the uprising (this didn't work out as Stapleton hoped; when Frank returned to Nevis he fled to St. Kitts after ten weeks, claiming—whether true or false—that he feared for his life. After that, he vanishes from the record).[42]

In the class and racial plantation systems of Jamaica, there was less of a place for nonelite white women. Although some white servants were valued in the early stages of plantation development, planters were generally reluctant to hire

---

40. Burnard, "A Failed Settler Society," 67.

41. Stephanie E. Jones-Rogers, *They Were Her Property: White Women as Slave Owners in the American South* (New Haven, CT: Yale University Press, 2019).

42. Keith Mason, "The Absentee Planter and the Key Slave: Privilege, Patriarchalism, and Exploitation in the Early Eighteenth-Century Caribbean," *William and Mary Quarterly* 70, no. 1 (2013): 79–102, 84.

white women, as an example from the 1670s illustrates.[43] Co-owner William Helyar was deeply opposed to having white women on his plantation, which led one woman to dress as a man in order to come to the plantation with her husband. When she arrived, she was greeted with the sentiment from the plantation owners that the plantation had "two [white] women . . . the Doctor's wife and the potter's, two filthy lazy sows good for nothing."[44] Because by custom white women didn't work in the fields, nonelite white women had limited ways to earn a living in Jamaica other than becoming mistresses to elite men.

The plantation system also shaped masculinity for white male planters, who stood at the top of the racial and gender hierarchy. Their economic and legal standing meant that they controlled not only their plantations, but also held important governmental positions as judges and colonial leaders. This did not mean, however, that white masculinity was either the same for all men or stable over the course of the eighteenth century. In early eighteenth-century England, landlords generally lived on their lands or were able to visit fairly often. This meant that landowners had a much more patriarchal relationship with the people on their lands; lords knew the tenants and renters and existed in a system of reciprocal obligations and duties. This was the "master-servant" relationship, where propertied men were masters and their social and economic inferiors were trusted servants.[45]

In the Caribbean, however, many of the plantation landlords were absentee; they lived in England and some of them never went to see their property. This created the problem of how to manage lands that were a long distance away. We see the difficulties in the case of Sir William Stapleton, who inherited estates in the Caribbean. Running the plantations through others whom he tried to bring into the patriarchal household model was difficult to do as an absentee landlord, primarily because of the time delay in communication; it could take weeks or months to send a letter via ship and receive a response. This drastically slowed down major decisions, such as who should be hired for key managerial posts, and was impractical for small decisions, most of which would be moot by the time the manager received a reply.

In the second half of the eighteenth century the patriarchal management system declined, and many planters implemented "gentry capitalism" where they ran plantations more like a business. In this, they "subjected their carefully vetted managers to closer scrutiny, insisted on improved systems of bookkeeping,

---

43. See also Lucille Mathurin Mair, *Historical Study of Women in Jamaica, 1655–1844*, edited with an introduction by Hilary McD. Beckles and Verene A. Shepherd (Jamaica: University of the West Indies Press, 2006), especially chapter 1, "The Arrivals of White Women."

44. Susan Dwyer Amussen, *Caribbean Exchanges: Slavery and the Transformation of English Society, 1640–1700* (Chapel Hill: University of North Carolina Press, 2007), 88.

45. Mason, "The Absentee Planter and the Key Slave," 83.

embraced new varieties of sugarcane and wider crop diversification, and encouraged limited amelioration of slave treatment and conditions."[46] This may seem like a minor shift, but it had larger social implications. In a patriarchal system, masters and servants had reciprocal relationships to each other—those farther up in the hierarchy owed at least a degree of care for those beneath them (even if this was lip service). However, it also meant that elites had greater involvement in the actions of those below them. If the man at the top of the hierarchy was knowledgeable about the goods his subordinates were making, and if he was available for consultation when questions/problems arose, then it could be a fairly efficient system. However, with the distances involved in the English landlords who attempted to manage Caribbean plantations from afar (and their general disinterest in running the plantations), this system broke down. Instead, British landowners had to reimagine their relationship to their Caribbean employees and slaves, and place experts as intermediaries to run the plantations. In doing so, masculine virtue shifted from being less a paternal/patriarchal role, and more a scientific/management role.

In shifting to a more managerial perspective, there were also class implications because landlords relied upon the numerous poor and middle-class men who were on the island. While some enslaved men served as managers, at the top of this managerial class were white men who were too poor to afford large plantations. These men had a host of different professions, from managing plantations, to serving as purchasing agents for planters, to running a variety of businesses primarily in the capital of Kingston. The most successful purchasing agents had (potentially kin) connections to the planter class that made them to trustworthy in the planter's eyes.

The majority of people of African origin in Jamaica were male, as we saw above in our discussion of the difference in numbers of enslaved men and women who were sold in West Africa. While slave buyers would purchase almost any slave who arrived without regard for whether they were a man or woman, the large plantation owners (who usually got first pick) preferred men. Plantation owners and managers preferred men because they saw sugar plantation work as physically demanding—one that men could do best.[47] This included not only planting the cane, but tasks during the "grinding season" that lasted from October to January, during which the sugar mills ran almost all day and night.

For men and women of African origin, life in Jamaica was likely to be brutal and short.[48] In Jamaica, as in other sugar-producing places, despite having a large

46. Mason, "The Absentee Planter and the Key Slave," 84.

47. Michael Tadman, "The Demographic Cost of Sugar: Debates on Slave Societies and Natural Increase in the Americas," *The American Historical Review*, 105, no. 5 (2000): 1543; 1551.

48. Randy Browne and Trevor Burnard have an article on the roles that enslaved men played in the creation of families in Berbice, British Guiana (on the northern coast of South America). See Randy M. Browne and Trevor Burnard, "Husbands and Fathers: The Family Experience of Enslaved Men in Berbice, 1819–1934," *New West Indian Guide* 91, 3-4 (2017):193-222.

influx of enslaved people from Africa, the slave population grew only very slightly. We see this in the numbers required for any slave population growth. In Jamaica, 575,000 new enslaved people were needed in order to increase the population by 250,000.[49]

Short life spans, along with the skewed gender ratio, meant that there was little natural increase of enslaved people. This meant that a large portion of enslaved people—about 80 percent—had been born in Africa (although in different areas).[50] The fact that there were so many more people who had come directly from Africa in Jamaica, and the fact that the majority of these were men, might have meant that sugar-producing areas had a higher degree of people who ran away, and more instances of "maroon" (groups of escaped slaves and their descendants) rebellions and wars on Jamaica.[51] Another implication is that because the enslaved people were predominantly young men who had been born in Africa, slave owners may have been more concerned about revolution, and therefore harsher in their punishments.

In the case of African-origin women, there is little evidence that plantation owners were hesitant to use women in the field—they might have preferred men, but they'd buy anyone (one of the most notorious methods of sale was the "scramble" in which enslaved people were kept in a pen and at a designated time buyers rushed into the pen and literally grabbed whomever they could). In fact, the majority of enslaved women in Jamaica were put to work in the fields.[52] We also see this in the hoes made in those Bristol iron foundries.

We see the presence of women in the fields in the sheer variety of hoes—there was not only a specific hoe that was designed to work best with a particular crop, there were also different sizes. Although it is later than our period under discussion here, we see in the *Illustrated Sheffield List* (Figure 2.1) for 1871 that there were a wide variety of different "Carolina hoes" in a range of sizes, from 0000 to 4.

The amount and variety of sizes of hoes illustrates that women and children were in the fields alongside men. In the Caribbean, plantation work was generally divided into three tiers of working gangs: one that did heavy labor, one that did lighter labor, and one for children age five to twelve.[53] While individual tasks may have differed, men and women shared many of the same working conditions. This

49. Trevor Burnard and Kenneth Morgan, "The Dynamics of the Slave Market and Slave Purchasing Patterns in Jamaica, 1655–1788," *William and Mary Quarterly* 58, no. 1 (2001): 205–228, 207.

50. Burnard and Morgan, "The Dynamics of the Slave Market," 207.

51. Tadman, "The Demographic Cost of Sugar," 1562.

52. Herbert S. Klein, "African Women in the Atlantic Slave Trade," in *Women and Slavery in Africa*, ed. Robertson and Klein, 29–38, 35.

53. Marietta Morrissey, *Slave Women in the New World: Gender Stratification in the Caribbean* (Lawrence: University Press of Kansas, 1989), 73.

80

THE ILLUSTRATED SHEFFIELD LIST.

Discount.	No.										
		CAROLINA HOES, &c.									
		Sizes..	6 by 7	6½ by 7½	7 by 8	7½ by 8½	8 by 9	8½ by 9½	9 by 10	9½ by 10½	inches.
			0000	000	00	0	1	2	3	4	
	2120	Carolina Hoe, Half-Bright, well Steeled	11/0	12/0	13/0	15/0	17/0	19/0	21/0	23/0	dozen.
	2121	Ditto, Cast Steel, Polished Back, Warranted to Cut as an Adze	17/0	18/6	20/0	23/0	26/6	29/6	32/6	35/6	"
	2122	Ditto, Bright Back, well Steeled	13/6	14/6	15/9	18/3	20/6	23/0	25/6	27/6	"
	2123	Ditto, Full Weight, Japanned or Self-Coloured, well Steeled	11/0	12/0	13/0	15/0	17/0	19/0	21/0	23/0	"
	2124	Ditto, Light Weight, Japanned or Self-Coloured, well Steeled	9/3	9/9	10/6	12/0	13/6	15/3	17/0	18/6	"
	2125	Ditto, Iron, Light Weight, Japanned or Self-Coloured	8/3	9/0	10/0	11/3	12/6	14/0	15/0	16/6	"
		Sizes..	5½ by 6½	6 by 7	6½ by 7½	7 by 8	7½ by 8½	8 by 9	8½ by 9½	9 by 10	inches.
			00	0	1	2	3	4	5	6	
	2126	**DEMERARA HOE, STEELED**	10/0	11/0	12/0	14/0	16/0	18/0	20/0	22/0	dozen.
	2127	Demerara Hoe, Light Weight, Steeled	8/3	9/9	10/9	12/3	13/3	14/6	16/3	18/0	"
		If extra Weight, 1/0 per dozen extra.									
		Sizes..			5¼ by 7	5¾ by 7½	6¼ by 8	6¾ by 8½	7¼ by 9	7¾ by 9½	inches.
					1	2	3	4	5	6	
	2128	P. and Crown West India Hoes			17/0	19/0	21/0	23/0	25/0	27/0	dozen.
		Sizes..				7 by 8	7½ by 8½	8 by 9	8½ by 9½	9 by 10	inches.
						0	1	2	3	4	
	2129	**PATENT RIVETTED EYED CAST STEEL CAROLINA HOE**				24/6	27/6	29/0	30/6	32/0	dozen.
		WEST INDIA HOES.									
		Sizes..	5 by 6½	5½ by 7	6 by 7½	6½ by 8	7 by 8½	7½ by 9	8 by 9½	8½ by 10	inches.
			00	0	1	2	3	4	5	6	
	2130	Bright Back, Full Weight, Steeled, West India Hoe	14/6	16/0	18/6	20/6	23/0	25/6	28/0	30/6	dozen.
	2131	Full Weight, Steeled, Half-Bright, ditto	12/0	13/0	15/0	17/0	19/0	21/0	23/0	25/0	"
	2132	Ditto Steeled, Japanned or Self-Coloured, ditto	11/0	12/0	13/6	15/6	17/6	19/0	20/9	22/6	"
	2133	Light Weight, Steeled, Japanned or Self-Coloured, ditto	12/0	13/0	15/0	17/0	19/0	21/0	23/0	26/0	"
		Sizes..	5 by 7	5½ by 7½	6 by 8	6½ by 7½	7 by 9	7½ by 9½	8 by 10		inches.
			00	0	1	2	3	4	5	6	
	2134	Brt. Polished Back, C.S. West India Hoe, Warntd. to cut as an Adze	15/0	17/0	19/0	21/0	23/0	25/0	27/0		dozen.
		Sizes..		5½ by 6½	6 by 7	6½ by 7½	7 by 8	7½ by 8½	8 by 9	8½ by 9½	inches.
	2135	Light Barbadoes or West India Hoe, all Iron		13/0	15/0	17/0	19/0	21/0	23/0	25/0	dozen.
		Sizes..		5½ by 6¾	6 by 7¼	6½ by 7¾	7 by 8¼	7½ by 8¾	8 by 9¼	8½ by 9¾	inches.
	2136	Frenchay West India Hoe, Heavy Steeled		15/0	17/0	19/0	21/0	23/0	25/0	27/0	dozen.
		Sizes..				4½ by 7½	5 by 7¾	5½ by 8¼	6 by 9	6½ by 9½	inches.
						1	2	3	4	5	
	2137	**STRONG HILLING OR RICE HOE, STEELED**				13/0	14/6	16/4	18/0	19/9	dozen.
	2138	Light Hilling or Rice Hoe, Steeled				11/6	13/0	14/6	16/0	17/9	"
		Sizes..				7 by 6½	7½ by 7½	8 by 7½	8½ by 8½		inches.
	2139	**COLUMBIA HOE, WELL STEELED**				14/6	17/0	19/6	22/0		dozen.

FIGURE 2.1 Edward Brooks, *The Illustrated Sheffield List, Entered at Stationers' Hall*, Eleventh and Twelfth Editions, Sheffield, 1871, p. 80 (earlier editions, like the 4th edition—undated—do not include plantation farm implements).

Source: Brookes, Edward. *The illustrated Sheffield list.* 11th and 12th eds. (1871), 80.

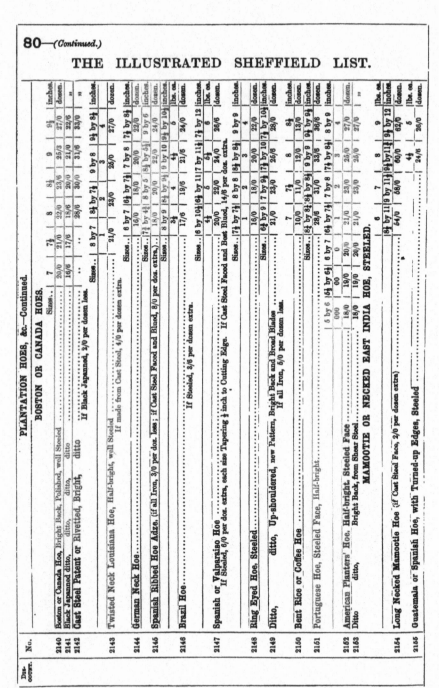

FIGURE 2.1 Continued

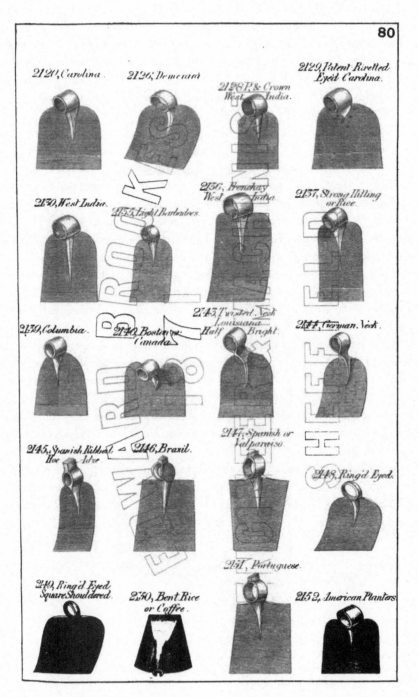

FIGURE 2.1 Continued

division of work, where women were in the fields alongside men and children, was a continuation of practices among some people along the Bight of Biafra, where all members of the family were involved in various stages of agricultural production, and men, women, and children used hoes.[54] Indeed, for many groups, men in the fields would have been seen as unusual instead of women, who were lauded for their agricultural skills and knowledge.

Slave life may have been similar to life in Africa in other ways as well. Enslaved people were generally given separate quarters from each other (at least during the development of plantations), and they were also generally allowed small plots to grow food. Many formed nuclear families for at least some period of time, until death or until one partner was sold. Some slave men even had several wives, and some women had several husbands.[55] Female-headed households were fairly common in slavery because in many places enslaved people were forbidden to marry and children followed the free or slave status of their mothers. Women generally gathered food, cooked, took care of the house, and made clothing.[56]

Other than these basics of slave life—mortality rates and working conditions—it is difficult to come to broad conclusions about slavery in the Americas, and you should look at the "Further Readings" section at the end of this chapter for more information on specific case studies. Historians disagree about many aspects of life for enslaved people, beginning with where they were from. While European slave buyers in Africa may have written down what groups enslaved people came from, there is no way to verify this information. Some historians take these labels seriously and argue that we can see links between African and American societies.[57] Other historians see the Middle Passage as a rupture, with slave societies in the Americas as too different for African societies to be replicated (such as having an almost exclusively male population on a sugar plantation or in the mines of Minas Gerais in Brazil).[58] In addition to these factors about enslaved people themselves, we also have the range of experiences based on which colony they lived in, and what time period.

---

54. Nwokeji, "African Conceptions of Gender," 56.

55. Morrissey, *Slave Women in the New World*, 89.

56. Morrissey, *Slave Women in the New World*, 48–9.

57. See for example Gwendolyn Midlo Hall, *Slavery and African Ethnicities in the Americas: Restoring the Links* (Chapel Hill: University of North Carolina Press, 2005); Jennifer L. Morgan, *Laboring Women: Reproduction and gender in New World Slavery* (Philadelphia: University of Pennsylvania Press, 2004).

58. See for example Kathleen J. Higgins *"Licentious Liberty" in a Brazilian Gold-Mining Region: Slavery, Gender, and Social Control in Eighteenth Century Sabará, Minas Gerais* (University Park: Penn State University Press, 1999); Michael A. Gomez, *Exchanging Our Country Marks: The Transformation of African identities in the Colonial and Antebellum South* (Chapel Hill: University of North Carolina Press, 1998).

We must also remember that not all people of color in Jamaica were enslaved; women such as Amey Crooks, a "free mulatto spinster" who lived in Jamaica during the 1700s, owned land that she was able to pass down to her children and grandchildren, along with twenty slaves. In many cities across the Caribbean and US South, women held a significant portion of the wealth of the community of free black people. This accumulation of assets allowed free black women to create spaces for both themselves and the community at large where they had control, and that were separate from potentially dangerous white spaces.[59]

The End of the Slave Trade: England and Abolition

Leaving the Caribbean behind, our ship *Clio* returns to its home port in England. By the end of the eighteenth century, it might have landed in a port that was rife with abolitionist sentiment, one where groups like the Society for Effecting the Abolition of the Slave Trade was formed. In the late eighteenth century and early nineteenth centuries, France, Great Britain, and the United States abolished the international slave trade, although slavery itself persisted in European colonies, the United States, and parts of Latin America until the late nineteenth century.

In the mid-eighteenth century, the abolitionist movement used gendered language to advance their cause. We see this in Josiah Wedgwood's famous 1789 drawing "Am I Not a Man and a Brother?" (Figure 2.2). Wedgwood (who was head of the Wedgwood ceramics company) had cameos created with this image, and it was widely distributed in Britain and the United States. Here, abolitionists were attempting to humanize enslaved people, arguing that enslaved people were not property, but *men* and potentially part of a community of fellow Christian believers. Although historians differ on the effect of the image and whether it was liberating (by pointing out the fundamental humanity of enslaved people, contrasted with the inhumanity of the chains), or whether it reinforced African subjugation (by showing a figure begging on his knees, passively asking Europeans and Americans for freedom), the gendered aspects of the image are clear.[60] In the context of European racial- and class-based masculinity, where only financially independent white men had full citizenship rights and everyone else was a legal and political dependent, even allowing slave men entry into the category of manhood could be a radical act.

As the 1700s progressed, we also see a change in what the British norms for masculinity, which bolstered abolitionist sentiment. For example, when

---

59. Erin Trahey, "Among Her Kinswomen: Legacies of Free Women of Color in Jamaica" *The William and Mary Quarterly*, 76, no, 2 (April 2019): 257-288.

60. See Marcus Wood, *The Horrible Gift of Freedom: Atlantic Slavery and the Representation of Emancipation* (Athens: University of Georgia Press, 2010), and Sidiya Hartman, *Lose Your Mother: A Journey Along the Atlantic Slave Route* (New York: FSG, 2008).

FIGURE 2.2 Josiah Wedgwood "Am I Not a Man and a Brother?" (1789).
Source: "Am I not a man and a brother?" 1837. Library of Congress, LC-USZC4-5321.

Thistlewood arrived in Jamaica in 1750, British culture emphasized the male "rake" who indulged his desires of all kinds, including sex. Historians Trevor Burnard and Richard Follet state that the image of a rake was of assertive raw male sexuality . . . [rakes] demonstrated . . . their homo-social status as men of honour. Masculinity, in particular, was associated with sexual dominance."[61]

---

61. Burnard and Follet, "Caribbean Slavery," 433.

Over the course of the eighteenth century, masculinity in Britain gradually moved to focus instead on men who were "sensible" (as they used that word), where men could be emotional, sensitive, and have sympathy with other human beings. In the process, men became more oriented toward the family; marriage promoted virtue and men were fathers and patriarchs, while women were mothers and softened the "harsh" edges of their husbands.

This extended to ideas of empire. The British intellectual Edmund Burke argued that British subjects (including colonized people) should be part of families if they were going to be part of civil society. As part of this shift, Jamaica and slave societies became increasingly out of step with British society, and were stained with a reputation as not only places where slave families were dismantled or prevented from forming, but also places where white men exercised "unnatural, unhealthy, and deviant" behaviors.[62] By 1800, white men like Thistlewood, who had multiple sexual partners were more likely to be denounced than celebrated in Britain.

We also see the connections between gender and abolition in the sugar boycott in 1791–1792. Abolitionists began a publicity campaign to try to connect sugar use to slavery by making sugar synonymous with slavery. One of the ways they did this was through the metaphor of bodily fluids and consumption. We see this in one of the most popular abolitionist pamphlets of the time, William Fox's 1791 *An Address to the People of Great Britain, on the Utility of Refraining from the Use of West India Sugar and Rum*. Fox stated that "the laws of our country may indeed prohibit us the sugar cane, unless we receive it through the medium of slavery. They may hold it to our lips, steeped in the blood of our fellow creatures, but They [sic] cannot compel us to accept the loathsome portion."[63] Fox even argued that eating sugar was equivalent to being a cannibal: "In every pound of sugar used," he said, "we may be considered as consuming two ounces of human flesh."[64] To eat sugar, then, was to consume the body and blood of enslaved people, becoming "savage" cannibals—an image that Europeans tended to reserve for colonized peoples.

The sugar boycott was also gendered in that it particularly targeted women. In 1828, one pamphleteer stated that a woman's "strong feelings and quick sensibilities, especially qualify her, not only to sympathise [sic] with suffering, but also to plead for the oppressed."[65] Indeed, sugar boycott advocates pointed to women's

---

62. Burnard and Follet, "Caribbean Slavery," 445–47.

63. William Fox, *An Address to the People of Great Britain, on the Utility of Refraining from the Use of West India Sugar and Rum* (London, 1791), Internet Archive, https://archive.org/details/addresstopeople00foxw, 4.

64. Fox, *An Address*, 5.

65. Elizabeth Coltman, *Appeal to the Hearts and Consciences of British Women* (Leicester, 1828), Google books, https://books.google.com/books?id=5jRcAAAAcAAJ&pg=PA4#v=onepage&q&f=false, 3.

sentimentality as one of the reasons that women were swayed by abolitionist arguments. In *An Address to Her Royal Highness the Dutchess* [sic] *of York, Against the Use of Sugar* an anonymous author argued that "the heaven-born daughters of our isle [Britain], with all the delicate sensibility which is their distinguishing characteristic, were pierced to the heart with the sufferings of the oppressed African; and with a fortitude which domes them the highest honour, refused to enjoy those sweets, which they supposed to be the price of blood."[66] For the British public at large, women's sympathy and emotional qualities made them both more able to—and more susceptible to—imagine the virtues of abolitionist arguments.

The abolitionist movement gained strength in the late eighteenth century, and by the start of the nineteenth century countries that had been substantially engaged in the slave trade, such as England and the United States, began to make the transatlantic slave trade illegal (although the domestic slave trade would persist for much longer). While this stopped much of the volume of Africans being transported to the Americas, slavery continued to shape the lives of millions of people in Brazil, the Caribbean, and the southern United States.

Conclusion

As we have seen in the course of this chapter, gender, race, and class all played a part in the expansion of European formal colonies in the Caribbean. At each step of our journey on our imaginary ship *Clio*, we've observed the different ways that gender entwined with transatlantic trade. In the British Isles, this influence was largely felt through the shifting patterns of work, as production was gradually shifted out of the household and into centralized locations (even if these processes were not mechanized, as they soon would be in the industrial revolution). In West Africa, gender influenced not only the types of societies that Europeans and Africans created, but also the gender disparity in the transatlantic slave trade. In Jamaica, we examined some of the implications of this disproportion for enslaved Africans. We also looked at the ways that the slave plantation system influenced European gender norms. Finally, we turned our attention to the abolitionist movement, and examined the ways that gender influenced the rhetoric and participation of British people.

It is important to note that unlike the formal governmental colonization that we saw in Chapter 1, the spread of formal colonization here was through commodities. In the 17th and 18th centuries, European states did not have formal holdings in West Africa. Instead, France, Britain, and the Netherlands generally

---

66. Quoted in Charlotte Sussman, "Women and the Politics of Sugar, 1792," *Representations* 48 (Autumn, 1994): 48–69, 59.

expanded their influence through trade and semi-private corporations such as the British East India Company, Royal African Company, and Dutch East India Company. This meant that the power dynamics were (as we see in this chapter), slightly different from Spanish formal state imposition of laws and religion in Chapter 1. In the transatlantic trade, Europeans were on a much more equal footing with non-Europeans in some geographic locations, and a much less equal footing in others. As we move forward into chapter 3, keep these two examples of imperial power relationships in mind, because we will encounter a third type of power relationship in settler colonialism and the creation of spaces.

FURTHER READING

Amussen, Susan Dwyer. *Caribbean Exchanges: Slavery and the Transformation of English Society, 1640–1700*. Chapel Hill: University of North Carolina Press, 2007.

Berry, Daina Ramey, and Leslie M. Harris, eds. *Sexuality and Slavery: Reclaiming Intimate Histories in the Americas*. Athens: University of Georgia Press, 2018.

Burnard, Trevor. "Evaluating Gender in Early Jamaica, 1674–1784." *History of the Family* 12, no. 2 (2007): 81–91.

Ipsen, Pernille. "'The Christened Mulatresses': Euro-African Families in a Slave-Trading Town." *The William and Mary Quarterly* 70, no. 2 (April 2013): 371–98.

Lussana, Sergio. *My Brother Slaves: Friendship, Masculinity, and Resistance in the Antebellum South*. Lexington: University Press of Kentucky, 2016.

Morgan, Jennifer. *Laboring Women: Reproduction and Gender in New World Slavery*. Philadelphia: University of Pennsylvania Press, 2004.

3

GENDER AND IMPERIAL SPACES IN FRENCH ALGERIA AND INDOCHINA

In 1834, the French artist Eugène Delacroix presented a painting titled *The Women of Algiers in their Apartment* (*Femmes d'Algers dans leur Appartment*). Take a moment to examine the painting in Figure 3.1, as you would any other primary source. Remember that as primary sources, paintings present an editorialized view of their subjects. Instead of using words or numbers, as written sources do, the information in a painting comes through the subject matter, the positioning of those subjects, and the use of light, shadow, and color. In this case, Delacroix depicted three women sitting on the floor in their harem, lavishly dressed in silks and jewels. The style of their dress was North African rather than European—they were wearing pants and generally loose-fitting garments, although two of the seated women had sections of their upper chests and arms exposed. They were in a relaxed pose; two of them have taken off their slippers. In the middle of them was a hukkah, a water pipe used for smoking tobacco. The seated women were light-skinned, in contrast to their dark-skinned servant, who was exiting the room on the right side of the painting. While three of the women had their gaze averted, either focused on each other or with their eyes cast down, the woman on the far right looked toward the viewer, returning the gaze. The image was one of soft-focus intimacy, in warm tones of yellow, gold, and red, giving the viewer a privileged glimpse into a space that was designated as all-female and off-limits to the public.

The Women of Algiers is important because of its place in the study of imperialism and history. In his groundbreaking 1978 book *Orientalism*, Edward Said marked the early and mid-nineteenth century as a turning point in the ways that Europeans (and people in the "West" more generally) viewed people whom they defined as "Orientals" or people in the "East."[1] During the early and mid-nineteenth century, Western academics, government officials, painters, novelists, and other intellectuals constructed a series of stereotypes that characterized what the

---

1. As we will see, this idea of Oriental/East was a bit slippery in terms of geographic location. Then, as today, European/Americans tend to refer to the East as sometimes being the same as Islamic groups/nations (which range from North Africa to Indonesia), sometimes Asia more broadly (from India to Japan), and sometimes Arabic (groups of people in what we call the Middle East).

FIGURE 3.1 Eugène Delacroix, *Femmes d'Algers dans leur Appartment*, 1834.
Source: WomenofAlgiers/Wikipedia

East was like. For our purposes, there are two aspects of Orientalism that are important. One is that this was a binary opposition—in other words, the East was everything the West was not. Second, this process was deeply gendered. Although Said didn't delve very deeply into gender in Orientalism, subsequent scholars have examined the role that women and ideas of gender played in the creation of East and West. The general stereotype was that European men were logical, skeptical, rational, and inclined toward technology, engineering, and science. In contrast, Oriental men were illogical, unable to draw simple and obvious conclusions from clear facts, superstitious, and often contradicted themselves.[2] Europeans portrayed Eastern women, as we see in *The Women of Algiers*, as sequestered, sexual objects who were oppressed, bored, and lazy. However, European women also perpetuated stereotypes of the downtrodden Eastern woman in order to advance their own claims to political power.[3] Metropolitan leaders and thinkers in Europe (and at the end of the 1800s, in the United States) used these types of gendered

2. I have drawn this list from Said's citation of Lord Cromer. See Edward Said, *Orientalism*, 1978, 38. The original source is the Earl of Cromer, *Modern Egypt* (New York: The Macmillan Company, 1916), https://archive.org/details/modernegypt00crom.

3. Antoinette Burton, *Burdens of History: British Feminists, Indian Women, and Imperial Culture, 1865–1915* (Chapel Hill: University of North Carolina Press, 1994).

stereotypes to portray colonized peoples not only antithetical to the modern and forward-thinking West, but also as in need of Western aid and guidance.

In this chapter, we will focus on the case studies of the French in Algeria and Indochina to examine the ways that gender influenced Orientalist ideas that shaped imperialism. France began military action in Algeria in 1830, primarily as a way to solidify political support at home. While the French King Charles X (who had ordered the invasion) was deposed two weeks later, the French public generally approved of involvement in Algeria, and supported both an ongoing war of expansion and French settlement. In the case of Indochina, French influence began with Catholic missionaries, and from the 1850s to 1900s France intervened in the region periodically under the guise of protecting missionaries from repression and persecution by Vietnamese rulers. In 1862, the Vietnamese government ceded territory to France, a trend that continued with different rulers in the surrounding regions, until by 1907 France controlled Vietnam (Cochinchina, Annam, and Tonkin), along with Cambodia and Laos, which collectively became French Indochina (hereafter Indochina). Although Algeria and Indochina were widely apart geographically (see the map 3.1), they were both incorporated into the French political sphere to some extent. As we will see, the geographic distance between France and Indochina meant that it had a different relationship to the French body politic than in Algeria, which was just across the Mediterranean Sea from France.

In order to examine the ways that gender influenced settler colonialism, we are going to look at a series of "spaces." I put spaces in quotes here because I mean not only physical places, but also the space of communities and groups. We might think of these as the entities that people construct within a physical space. For example, a school campus can be the container for a space of education, in which students, faculty, and staff come together to complete specific types of tasks, who are bound to each other in certain ways as a community, and who maintain an allegiance to each other as members of that community even after they no longer meet there (in other words, after students become alumni). We can extend this type of educational community to schools across the nation, which have similar schedules and rhythms to each other, meaning that there is a very wide community of people who are involved in creating a broad educational space. Furthermore, since we all have a similar (enough) experience of this educational space, we might think of this as a universal experience—our understanding of educational space is what education naturally is, and what it should (or shouldn't) be.

French imperial officials attempted to create these same types of communities within different physical settings. The spaces that we are going to focus are in cities, hill station European communities in the tropics, harems, and European homes. In each of these settings, French reformers and colonial official's ideas of gender worked alongside race and nationality in order to dictate what roles men and women should play, and how non-European people violated those norms (according to French officials).

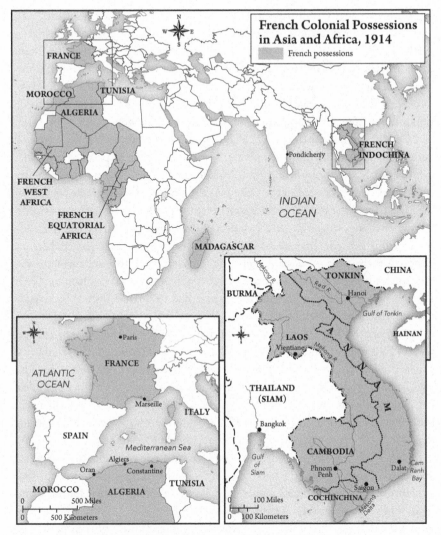

MAP 3.1 French Colonial Possessions in Asia and Africa, 1914

The City Itself: Algiers and Hanoi

Before we embark on our case studies, we need a brief review of cities during the late 1700s and early 1800s. In this time period, many cities around the world were in flux. In Europe, the growing network of transportation (first via water and canals, and then via steam) connected cities to ever-widening circumferences of the surrounding countryside. These transportation lines brought not only goods but people from ever-lengthening distances away, swelling the populations of cities and causing an increasing gap between the wealthy and the poor. At the same time, the lack of clean water supplies, and the increase in sewage, caused hardship and death for many people—particularly the poor—as waterborne diseases such as dysentery and later cholera swept through cities during the warm summer months.

The new modern infrastructure was a striking contrast with the old, medieval remnants in many European cities. Fires were relatively common in these places, partly because many of the buildings were constructed with wood that made them catch fire relatively easily, and because without a network of water supplies, fires were difficult to put out once started. Over the course of the 1600s and 1700s, significant sections of major European cities burned: Glasgow, Scotland in 1652; London in 1666; Northampton, England, in 1675; Bergen, Norway in 1702; and Copenhagen, Denmark in 1728 (European cities were far from alone in experiencing devastating fires. Major fires destroyed significant parts of Nagasaki, Edo/Tokyo, Kyoto, Boston, and New York during this period as well). These fires tended to be concentrated in the older parts of cities, and while tragic because of the loss of life and property, provided city planners with a blank slate on which to rebuild or change the layout and function of those areas of the city. Many simply rebuilt along the same lines as the structures in the past, preserving street layouts, although there were occasional nods by the government to implement restrictions on building materials (for example, after a fire in Dorset, England, in 1731, Parliament passed an act that reconstruction had to be done in less flammable materials such as brick and tile).

One place that hadn't burned was Paris. In the early 1800s, much of the medieval parts of Paris were still intact, with their narrow streets, old and unhealthy buildings, and lack of infrastructure. By the 1840s, reformers in European and American cities were beginning to attack these types of conditions as in need for reform. In addition to a general urge to remodel, French rulers had an additional incentive; residents in the center of Paris had found it easy to blockade the narrow medieval streets during the 1848 Revolution using paving stones they ripped up from the street.

In the 1830s and 1840s, then, French officials were very conscious of the benefits and drawbacks of cities, and what a "modern" city should look like, with it's infrastructure of sewers and water supplies, it's network of transportation for trains and roads for horses, and it's architecture for public and private buildings. In the case of Paris, we see this in the efforts to transform the center of the city, spearheaded by the architect and urban designer, Georges-Eugène Haussmann. In the 1850s and 1860s, Haussmann embarked on massive building projects in Paris, demolishing medieval neighborhoods to create wide boulevards, urban green spaces, and symmetrical housing blocks, which all encompassed new sewers and water supplies.

At the same time that French rulers and urban planners such as Haussmann were thinking about what made a city good/modern, and what made it bad/a relic of the past, the French government was encountering the reconstruction of another city— Algiers. Once the period of immediate pacification in urban centers in Algeria was over (and it is important to remember that the French government's rule was largely limited to urban areas), French military and government officials began to build and rebuild cities, making them into military and administrative colonial centers.

In these cities colonial officials held to two main ideas: that public and private spaces should be separated from each other; and that modern European architecture was preferable, with its straight lines and visible public spaces, and its hidden public infrastructure of sanitation and water supplies. This reflected the same sorts of Orientalist ideas as we saw with the Delacroix painting—to be Oriental was to be hidden and secretive (female), while Western was to be public and modern (male).

One of the main ways that French officials attempted to transform Algiers —and later Hanoi—was to embark on massive building projects that both rational-ized the city into different zones with different functions, and which allocated certain areas for predominantly French or Algerian and Vietnamese usage. In the case of Algiers, the city sits on the Mediterranean Sea and has a relatively flat coastal area, with a hill rising above. In the Ottoman period, the hill (al-Jabal) was generally populated by the elite, and was made up of about fifty small neigh-borhoods. The lower area of the city (al-Wati'), near the port, was composed of businesses, homes, military barracks, and major mosques. When the French army arrived they began to destroy the city, burning the archives, looting homes, and seizing buildings. In 1832, the military also began erasing the Muslim areas of Algiers by doing things such as converting Ketchaoua Mosque into a Christian cathedral and relocating Muslim cemeteries in order to build roads. They also de-molished the central core of the city.[4]

French officials do not seem to have hesitated much in this process, because they don't appear to have viewed the buildings they tore down as being functional or at-tractive. The author of a report from the time stated that the French "demolish many ugly shops, several houses, and promptly obtain a very useful space for the troops, the carriages, the markets."[5] Under plans made by the government, officials destroyed the al-Sayyida Mosque (including its minaret), but after an outcry from the Algerian Muslim population they were prevented from demolishing the al-Jadid Mosque, the other main historic mosque in the lower area of the city. In its place, plans called for a type of rational and regularized layout of the city, what historian Zeynep Çelik has described as "symmetry and regularity (to be enhanced by landscaping), continu-ous façades with arcades on the ground level, and buildings whose functions were intertwined with the French presence, such as a government palace and a theater."[6] Although these specific buildings were not completed, the goal here was clear—to erase supposedly Oriental chaos with European order. In case Algerians were in doubt about the purpose of these demolitions, in 1845 French colonial officials placed a statue of the Ferdinand Philippe, the duke of Orléans (who had fought in the French-Algerian wars), in one of the main crossroads of the lower city, right in front of the al-Jadid Mosque and facing the old city. On the minaret of the mosque,

---

4. Clancy-Smith, "Exoticism, Erasures, and Absence," 24; 26.

5. René Lespés, *Alger: Étude de géographie et d'historie urbaines* (Paris: Librarie Félix Alcan, 1930), 205. Quoted in Zeynep Çelik, " Historic Intersections: The Center of Algiers," in Çelik, Clancy-Smith, and Terpak, *Walls of Algiers*, 198–226, 201.

6. Çelik, "Historic Intersections," 203–04.

French officials placed a clock tower, transforming it into a secular structure, with an emphasis on rational and modern time rather than the eternal religious.[7]

French officials saw the old city in Hanoi much the same way—as historian Michael Vann states, as a "labyrinthine layout ... an alien maze."[8] They viewed Vietnamese structures in Hanoi as relics of the past, and while they thought that pagodas and temples might be visually appealing, they were also symbols of "lost civilizations."[9] In their view, French buildings would be more modern and permanent. This was reflected in the building materials: most of the structures in pre–French Hanoi were created from wood with thatched roofs, and the French attempted to build in stone or brick.[10] And indeed, several years of intensive fighting between French forces and the resistance group the Black Flag had left much of Hanoi in ruins by the time the French began to permanently occupy it in July 1884. As Raoul Bonnal, the first *Résident* (a type of diplomatic official) of Hanoi stated, "Hanoi presents the sad image of a dead city."[11]

French officials and architects in Hanoi also did much the same as those in Algiers (and in Paris), demolishing parts of the city and reordering it. In 1886, Paul Bert arrived in Hanoi as the first civilian administrator for the city, and he transformed the city into a French colonial space. As had the architects and city planners in Algiers, Bert overlaid a grid onto the existing map of Hanoi, demolishing buildings and moving inhabitants who stood in the way.

This massive renovation of urban centers was not just part of eliminating a chaotic/Eastern/feminine/obsolete sense of these cities. Part of the point of these urban design changes was to change what was visible and what was invisible—the parts of the city that French officials thought should be public and what should be private. For many officials, "public" in a colonial context meant male. By the 1930s the French male population in Hanoi had grown from soldiers, military officials, and high-level diplomatic and administrative men to include other professions such as engineers (who supervised public infrastructure works), physicians, and a growing number of rubber plantation owners and merchants.[12] European women in public government spaces were relatively rare. Although the French colonial administration did reserve some clerical positions and employment opportunities for women, these were generally set aside for widows and fatherless daughters of colonial officials.

---

7. Çelik, " Historic Intersections," 205–06.

8. Michael G. Vann, "White City on the Red River: Race, Power, and Culture in French Colonial Hanoi, 1872–1954," PhD diss., University of California–Santa Cruz, 1999, 31.

9. Vann, "White City on the Red River," 28.

10. Vann, "White City on the Red River," 29.

11. Raoul Bernnal cited in Gouvernement Géneral de l'Indochine-Direction de l'Instruction Publique, *L'Oeuvre de la France en Indochine: La Paix Français* (Hanoi: Imprimerie de l'Extrene Orient, 1927), 5; cited in Vann, "White City on the Red River," 63.

12. Vann, "White City on the Red River," 509–10.

Women-owned business in this male space of Hanoi were also rare, and tended to be limited to fields such as cooking and needlework.[13] Women business owners at times received a hostile reception from male merchants, who viewed them as competition. Anger was particularly aimed at women who were married, and thus were viewed to have the ability to survive on their husband's income. For example, in 1897 the Saigon chamber of commerce wrote to the governor of Cochinchina that local merchants strongly opposed the wives of civil servants setting up businesses. The governor sided with the business owners, and wrote to one civil servant telling him to close down his wife's shop.[14] However, at the same time, colonial groups who were attempting to get women to emigrate to Indochina argued that girls would need to know not only home economic skills, but also the same subjects that boys were offered in the event that they had to run their husband's businesses during his illness or upon his death.[15]

A potential point of contention between public and private spaces within cities were cafés. On one hand they were quasi home-like, with a connection to feminine tasks such as making and serving food, thus serving as a potential connection to French culture and "home." On the other hand, they were not private, but were open to the public. For example, Madame de Beire ran a famous café in Hanoi in the early days of the French presence (a colonial joke was "that the first thing the Spanish did when they colonized an area was to build a church; the English would set up a market; and the French would build a *café*"). Madame Beire was the only French woman in Hanoi for many years, and had even gained a legendary reputation by helping to defend French forces from the Black Flags.[16] Beire's café—and cafés in general—provided a distinctly French space, attempting to serve French dishes and catering to a French clientele.[17]

However, officials also saw cafés as a potential cover for women being too much in public and as potential prostitutes. In July 1910, the police commissioner complained to the mayor of Hanoi that Valaques (women from the Wallachia region of Romania) were causing what he called "scandals" by being out in public at night and soliciting potential clients. Nevertheless, the Wallachian women proved difficult for officials to deal with because they also ran cafés. Because they had a separate income that could explain their self-support, and were not registered as prostitutes with the officials, it was difficult for the vice squad to prove

---

13. Marie-Paule Ha, *French Women and the Empire: The Case of Indochina* (Oxford: Oxford University Press, 2014) 147–49 (these included "food-related services, such as cafés and restaurants, and retail stores of clothing and dry goods," 148).

14. Ha, *French Women and the Empire*, 149.

15. Ha, *French Women and the Empire*, 51.

16. Vann, "White City on the Red River," 67.

17. Ha, *French Women and the Empire*, 148.

that they were prostitutes. Instead of charging them, the police commissioner evidently put surveillance on the café. The agent in charge of this stated that the women wore "indecent and provocative clothes" and that one of the women "was on her veranda rocking on a chair with her legs pushing against the pillars, and as they were raised to the same level as her head, you could see her legs above the knees."[18] These unfeminine actions, which took place in view of the public, caused the police to arrest three of the women and to bring them into a clinic for medical examinations, looking for something such as a venereal disease that could be evidence of prostitution (they were all found to be healthy).[19]

In keeping with the view of most Oriental women as being hypersexualized, French officials also tended to view Algerian and Vietnamese women who were visible in cities as likely prostitutes. In Algeria, Edouard Duchesne's 1853 study *On Prostitution in the City of Algiers Since the Conquest (De la prostitution dans la ville d'Alger depuis la conquête)* attempted to give an overview of the situation. As historian Julia Clancy-Smith states, Duchesne argued that the significant numbers of Arab prostitutes in the city was due to the "debased moral state of the indigenous population, the product of Islamic legal and sociosexual practices" in which girls were married young and had multiple pregnancies before their husbands divorced them for younger women.[20] Duchesne also saw these women as having to resort to prostitution due to their own moral failings—their dislike of work and their lack of education. However, he also viewed these women as undesirable and unattractive; the women's appeal to French soldiers was simply in "their strangeness and newness."[21]

This idea of "Oriental" women as simultaneously hypersexualized and as victims of exploitative patriarchy was cemented by images of women created by European artists (such as Delacroix in *Women of Algiers*) and later, photographers such as Félix-Jacques Antoine Moulin. Moulin arrived in Algeria 1856 with the financial and logistical backing of the French government, and created hundreds of photographs of Arab prostitutes (although his mission was officially to document the ways that French rule had benefitted North Africa).[22] Photos of veiled women in public, and the harem with clothed and unclothed women sequestered inside, were even

---

18. Quoted in Isabelle Tracol-Huynh, "The Shadow Theater of Prostitution in French Colonial Tonkin: Faceless Prostitutes under the Colonial Gaze," *Journal of Vietnamese Studies* 7, no. 1 (2012): 10–51, 18–19.

19. Tracol-Huynh, "The Shadow Theater of Prostitution," 19.

20. Julia Clancy-Smith, "Islam, Gender, and Identities: French Algeria," in *Domesticating the Empire: Race, Gender, and Family Life in French and Dutch Colonialism*, ed. Julia Clancy-Smith and Frances Gouda (Charlottesville: University of Virginia Press, 1998), 154–174, 160.

21. Edouard Adolphe Duchesne, *De la prostitution dans la ville d'Alger depuis la conquête* (Paris, 1853), 78. Quoted in Clancy-Smith, "Islam, Gender, and Identities," 161.

22. This work was not uncontroversial—Moulin was jailed for a month in 1851 for "producing images 'so obscene that even to pronounce the titles ... would be to omit an indecency.'" Quoted in The Metropolitan Museum of Art, "'Divine Perfection': The Daguerreotype in Europe and America," *Metropolitan Museum of Art Bulletin* 45, no. 4 (Spring 1999): 40–46.

sold as postcards, which were inexpensive ways to spread the alleged exoticism and oppression of Arab-looking women (I use "Arab-looking" here as it is important to note that most of these images were staged and used models who were not necessarily Muslim or Arabic, despite the postcard captions of "Moorish").[23]

In addition to painters and photographers, novelists such as Hector France also presented a view of North-African women as hypersexual. France's 1886 work *Musk, Hashish, and Blood* (a work of fiction despite it's appearance as a travel narrative) contained descriptive scenes of the narrator's sexual exploits with the women of the Awlad Na'il tribe, some of whom traded sex for money in order to gain funds for a dowry. While Europeans had known of the Awlad Na'il tribe since the Crusades, the 1800s marked a renewed interest in these "libertine Saharan beauties" in works that purported to be scientific but were generally more voyeuristic and pornographic.[24]

Europeans also tended to characterize Vietnamese women as simultaneously hypersexual and victims. Dr. Andre Joyeaux, the municipal doctor of Hanoi, wrote a study of prostitution in the city in 1930. In this tract, he spent several pages articulating the differences between Vietnamese, Japanese, Chinese, and European prostitutes. In his description of Asian prostitutes, he made further distinctions of them as submissive, songstresses, and concubines of Europeans. The author of a 1942 report labeled Chinese prostitutes as "recalcitrant par excellence to all regulations" and mixed-race prostitutes as "unstable and above all undisciplined."[25] This was an attempt to attach a sexual stereotype to racial categories. As these examples show, race played a key role in the ways that Europeans viewed the "feminine" qualities of Asian women and their sexuality vis-à-vis European men.

"Public women" (as prostitutes were sometimes called) were troubling to colonial officials not only because they were in public spaces, but also because they might be invisible to the eyes of the state. We see this in Tonkin when officials passed a law in the 1860s that prostitutes needed to be registered and subjected to periodic health inspections, in order to try to stop the transmission of venereal disease. In 1866 officials in Tonkin formed a vice-squad police whose responsibility was to find prostitutes, make sure that they were registered, take them to clinics, and lock them up there if the women were either not registered or were diagnosed with a venereal disease.[26] The officials particularly worried about women who were isolated, or *filles isolées*, who were not part of a brothel. Curiously, Tonkin brothels were a combination of visible and hidden. They were required have a lantern with the glass painted green (that needed to be lit from seven in the evening to five in the morning) and red house numbers. At the same time, however, the windows

23. Malek Alloula, *Colonial Harem*, translated by Myrna Godzich and Wlad Godzich (Minneapolis: University of Minnesota Press, 1986).

24. Clancy-Smith, "Islam, Gender, and Identities in French Algeria," 158.

25. Quoted in Tracol-Huynh, "The Shadow Theater of Prostitution," 35–36.

26. Tracol-Huynh, "The Shadow Theater of Prostitution," 12.

had to be kept closed at all times.[27] In this way, the establishments were easily identified (presumably making them easier to surveil or to use), while the people within them were hidden from view—a combination of visibility and invisibility.

Tropical Respite: Dalat Hill Station

At the end of the nineteenth century, reformers and colonial officials across the British the United States, and the French Empires, became concerned about what we see today as a curious paradox. According to the racial theories of the time, based heavily in social Darwinism, white European and US men were supposed to be the pinnacle of civilization—strong, intelligent, restrained, masculine caretakers. Yet these men were increasingly being diagnosed with a disease called neurasthenia or lack of "nerve force." In essence, some medical thinkers at the time thought of the body as a closed system. When blood went to one area to be used, such as the brain, it was "stolen" from another area of the body, such as the muscles for men or the reproductive organs for women. For men, this meant that too much use of the brain, without accompanying exercise, could lead to an "overtaxing" of the nerves and potential nervous breakdown. White European and American men's supposed intellectual strength, then, was also their greatest weakness.

The cure for neurasthenia was rest, and all across tropical colonies European empires set up towns at higher altitudes for male colonial officials and their families to "recover" from the heat and humidity that could put an additional strain on their nerves. For Indochina this was the hill station of Dalat (sometimes spelled Da Lat), 150 miles north and east of Saigon. Because Dalat was created in response to French vulnerability, particularly the susceptibility of French (men) to tropical disease, it was therefore slightly different to the examples of cities that we saw above. Hill stations were created by colonial governments as a not only a cure not only for the perils of a tropical climate, such as malaria (the altitude was generally too high for mosquitoes that carried the disease), but also as a cheaper solution to bringing colonial officials and their families back to the metropole for periodic rest and relaxation.

Hill stations were important because they mimicked European climates. Although humoral theories (in which climate influenced health) had been discredited by the 1800s, colonial officials still saw white bodies as being put under stress by tropical weather. As Paul Doumer (future president of France) wrote in a letter to the Minister of the Colonies in 1898, Dalat's "vivifying air, a temperate climate, analogous to some extent to Southern Europe's" was "capable . . . of restoring their health and vigor, altered by the humidity and heat of the lowlands."[28] Visitors particularly remarked upon the cool climate as beneficial

27. Tracol-Huynh, "The Shadow Theater of Prostitution," 20.

28. Quoted in Eric T. Jennings, *Imperial Heights: Dalat and the Making and Undoing of French Indochina* (Berkeley: University of California Press, 2011), 32.

to Europeans; a 1926 tourist guide stated that in Dalat "pure air excites the appetite. One feels the need for movement, physical exercise, and intellectual work utterly foreign to us in Saigon."[29] For colonial administrators, hill stations were not only about making colonial bureaucracy more efficient by becoming healthier, they also cut costs, as there would be fewer "repatriations" of French men and women back to France (the colonial government generally paid ship fare).

In addition to finding a climate that mimicked Europe, colonial officials also attempted to reproduce the home country through architecture and food. In Dalat two-story homes and public buildings prevailed and European fruits and vegetables could be grown, creating a more European diet (before the early 1900s most French in Saigon and Hanoi had to rely on canned foods shipped from France). There was a casino or *cercle* (although it was open less than a year before gambling was outlawed), a sports club, an arboretum, a hotel, and even a French *pâtisserie* (the Pâtisserie Dauphinoise). European housing in Dalat was also modeled after European villas, particularly those along the Côte d'Azur, as well as mountain villas from the Alps (see the photo of the Lang-Bian Palace Hotel in Figure 3.2). A hunting lodge provided a space from which European hunters could shoot big game such as tigers and elephants.[30]

While Dalat might have been conceived for French male colonial officials, over the course of the early twentieth century it increasingly became a residence for these men's families. A 1942 pamphlet explained that Dalat was to "allow women and children, the sick, those who suffer from the rigors of the Indochinese climate, to find reinvigoration, strength, and good health."[31] While this change of Dalat from masculine to a place for women and children took place over time, one of the key changes occurred in the 1910s and 1920s, when several schools were built. Like the town in general, these schools attempted to replicate French curriculum—all of the instruction was in French, the children ate the same types of food in the cafeteria as their metropolitan compatriots, and they took the same exams. In Dalat, French women became de facto heads of household, as their husbands were often working in cities such as Saigon or Hanoi. This allowed some women to have greater authority over their children and households than they might otherwise have had.

Domestic Spaces: The Harem and the European Home

One of the most important places for colonial officials in Algeria and Indochina was the home. This preoccupation with the home was partly because of its status as a site to enact culture. Colonial officials generally subscribed to the idea that the full conquest of Algeria could only take place if the family unit (in the home) was

29. Quoted in Jennings, *Imperial Heights*, 89.

30. Jennings, *Imperial Heights*, 84; 90–91; 131.

31. Quoted in Jennings, *Imperial Heights*, 132.

FIGURE 3.2 The Lang-Bian Palace hotel in the 1920s (the Vichy Governor General of Indochina, Jean Decoux, had the façade removed in 1943).
Source: Raymond Chagneau/Dalat Palace Hotel, 1920s/Wikipedia

broken up.[32] French officials disliked Arab houses on several levels. One reason was that they were generally closed to the street with an open courtyard within, which officials felt shifted the emphasis away from a visible public to a hidden internal focus. Terraces between houses also restricted some views and allowed others, and they seemed to facilitate secret communications between the inhabitants. A. M. Perrot's 1830 description of Algerian architecture labeled these houses as "jealous" and incorrectly attributed the "bizarre" allocation of space to Islam, mapping onto an idea from French philosopher Montesquieu that "in despotic states, each house is a separate empire."[33] Pierre Trémaux, a French architect who studied Algerian homes in the 1800s, argued that the grills on the windows gave the houses a prison-like appearance, and that they must have been placed there in order to keep the women and slaves from escaping.[34]

According to French officials, one of the key aspects of despotism was the presence of the harem. As we see from Delacroix's *Women of Algiers* (with which we started this chapter) and the positive reception that it enjoyed in France, French officials and the general public focused on the harem as a unique feature of Islamic life. In this it was either a source of curiosity, as in *Women of Algiers*, or

---

32. Zeynep Çelik, "A Lingering Obsession: the Houses of Algiers in French Colonial Discourse," in Çelik, Clancy-Smith, and Terpak, *Walls of Algiers*, 134–160, 19.

33. Quoted in Çelik, "A Lingering Obsession," 134.

34. Çelik, "A Lingering Obsession," 141.

more often a source of sexual fantasy for French men. At the root of this fascina-
tion with the harem were two interrelated facts: first, that Islamic people were
generally barred from writing about the harem, so there was a lack of information about that space in general; and second, that the women in the harem were
generally slaves.

In fact, most European depictions of the harem were pure fiction—they would
not have been allowed in that space to observe the things in their works of art.
While Delacroix had actually gone to Morocco with a French mission in the early
1830s, there are doubts about whether or not he visited a harem, and he painted
Women of Algiers in Paris, using Parisian women as his models for the women's
faces.[35] Other painters were even further removed from accuracy. Jean-Auguste-
Dominique Ingres never went to North Africa or the Eastern Mediterranean.
Instead, his works were based on accounts of travelers, particularly the memoir of
Lady Mary Wortley Montagu, wife of the British ambassador to Turkey, Ingres's
paintings are voyeuristic, presenting women (who would have been hidden from
the male gaze in real life) as nude and in sexually provocative poses (particularly
his painting *The Turkish Bath*).

This stereotype of the harem is important to understanding Orientalism because it formed one of the central features of Western views of the East: the idea
that women would be involuntarily cloistered, bored, and unable to participate
in the public sphere. The images by painters allowed European Westerners to gain
access to imaginary versions of these closed spaces, in order to see how "different" (at least in the imagination of the artist) and by extension inferior, those
spaces were.[36] The image of femininity within these spaces was, in the case of
male French painters and photographers, highly sexualized, unlike the ways that
European women were portrayed at the time.[37]

However, the idea that all Arab women were sequestered in harems, trapped and
bored, was a fiction. First, not all North African homes had harems. Harems generally existed in wealthy Muslim houses, and there were Jewish and Christian women
living in North Africa some of whom practiced sequestering or veiling (these were
the women most often used as models in the harem postcards), while others did not.

---

35. Roger Benjamin, *Orientalism: Delacroix to Klee* (Sydney: Art Gallery of New South Wales,
1997), 11. Art historian Todd Porterfield argues that many of the elements in the painting in
fact appeared in earlier works by French painters. We might therefore characterize Delacroix's
Women of Algiers as a mid-point of accuracy, based in his own (very limited) access and experience, but constructed later and from French elements.

36. In fact, the secrecy around harem life has generally meant that we have relatively few historical documents about them; they were generally a taboo subject.

37. For example, the French Realist school, including Gutave Courbet's *Young Women from
the Village* (1851–1852) and Edouard Manet's *Olympia* (1863), in which the model covers her
genitals. For more information on this movement see Ross Finocchio, "Nineteenth-Century
French Realism," *Metropolitan Museum of Art*, October 2004, https://www.metmuseum.org/
toah/hd/rlsm/hd_rlsm.htm.

In fact, a more accurate division of spaces (both household and more public) would be to consider them as gendered subspheres or subspaces. Men's spaces included homes, mosques, workplaces, markets, and dervish lodges, and women's spaces included harems, saints' tombs and shrines, recreational areas, and public baths.[38]

A second European misconception of harems was that they were full of wives. However, relatively few Muslim families could financially support multiple wives (which would make a harem necessary), or even the sequestration of one woman—women in many households had to be in public, earning wages. In fact, recent studies in late Ottoman Istanbul indicate that only 2.29 percent of married men were polygamous, and most of them had only two wives. For North Africa, research indicates that less than 5 percent of households were polygamous. The idea of the harem as a space where many wives congregated was therefore a European invention instead of a North African or Ottoman reality.[39]

Despite these facts, French reformers generally focused on the image of the harem and the repressed Arab woman as a rationale for intervention in Algerian domestic spaces. For example, French feminist Hubertine Auclert, who had founded a radical section of the feminist movement in France, had lived in Algeria for a number of years during the late 1880s and early 1890s. Auclert was highly critical of French colonialism, which she found to be racist, exclusionist, and anti-Semitic.[40] For Auclert, Arab women were the key symbol of the failure of French colonialism in Algeria because the French government had not intervened enough. Practices such as child marriage, the sale of brides, and polygamy had been left undisturbed, and women were therefore "little victims of Muslim debauchery."[41] Auclert argued that the French had a duty (as Julia Clancy-Smith states) to "turn harem inmates into voters. If Arab men sought access to the ballot box, so did Arab females who also aspired to be assimilated—to become Frenchwomen, freed from their cages, walled homes, and cloisters."[42] For some European women, taking up the cause of their "downtrodden sisters" was a way for them to gain political capital in the metropole. Arguing that they shared a bond with women in the colonies, these women argued that they needed to have a greater say in their European governments.[43]

Social reformers in France well into the early twentieth century not only continued the stereotypes of the nineteenth century—that Algerians and other

---

38. Schick, "The Harem as a Gendered Space," 72.

39. Schick, "The Harem as a Gendered Space," 71.

40. Clancy-Smith, "Islam, Gender, and Identities in French Algeria," 168.

41. Quoted in Clancy-Smith, "Islam, Gender, and Identities in French Algeria," 170.

42. Clancy-Smith, "Islam, Gender, and Identities in French Algeria," 170.

43. For work on British women, see Burton, *Burdens of History*. This was also the case in the United States. See Peggy Pascoe, *Relations of Rescue: The Search for Female Moral Authority in the American West, 1874–1939* (New York: Oxford University Press, 1990).

North Africans were backward and tyrannical—but also that North African homes were physically *unhealthy*. They complained that the lack of windows and openings onto the street created a lack of sunlight and fresh air, which allowed disease to spread. Reformers argued that this hidden world, left unchanged, was resistant to modernization and progress.[44]

Despite these reforming impulses, the structure of most homes in Algeria did not fundamentally change during either the late 1800s or the early 1900s. Many of the same types of tropes about veiling and sequestered women were also still very much present when the Algerian War of Independence erupted in 1954.[45]

While colonial officials saw the unreformed colonized home as a site of transmission for "backward" or repressive ideas, they also saw French colonial homes as a location to extend French influence to Algerian and Vietnamese people. At the turn of the nineteenth and early twentieth centuries colonial officials began to emphasize the role that French women could play as colonial agents.

In keeping with the theories of social Darwinism and race purity of the time, perhaps the most important role that officials envisioned for French women was as sexual partners to male colonial officials. While colonial officials in earlier periods had tended to see women from the local area as an asset for their language skills and social networks, the growing popularity of social Darwinism at mid-century meant that European masculinity and European racial separateness had to be maintained (to put it bluntly, no more mixed-race children).

However, most reformers did not directly come out and say that women should go to the colonies so they could get married and have sex with French men. Instead, officials and reformers couched it in terms of domesticity. As a Jesuit priest stated, "the French woman must also go to the colonies to help, console, and support her husband, to watch over his well-being and his health, to care for him in a thousand indispensable ways."[46] Frenchwomen would therefore solve the "danger" of male colonial officials, who could easily "go native" by adopting "native" sexual partners (leading to mixed-race children), wearing local dress, and adopting non-European ways of thought.

Two characters from Georges Groslier's 1928 novel *The Return to Clay (Le Retour á l'argile)* illustrate the feminine qualities Frenchwomen were expected to display—or not display—in the colonies at the time. The character of Simone Bertrand represents the idealized colonial woman—helpful to her husband, happy, practical, and uncomplaining. She was able to supervise workers on her

44. Janet Horne, "In Pursuit of Greater France: Visions of Empire among Musée social Reformers," in *Domesticating the Empire*, ed. Clancy-Smith and Gouda, 39.

45. See Todd Shepard, *The Invention of Decolonization: the Algerian War and the Remaking of France* (Ithaca, NY: Cornell University Press, 2006).

46. Marie-Paule Ha, *French Women & the Empire: The Case of Indochina* (Oxford: Oxford University Press, 2014), 54.

husband's rubber plantation just as easily as she socialized with other French colonial people. In contrast to Bertrand was Raymonde Rollin, who focused on her clothes and makeup, and her own thoughts and social activities. She complained about Indochina soon after arriving, and wanted to return to France. Her failure as a woman and a French colonial was evident when her husband abandoned her for a Vietnamese woman, and she was forced to leave Indochina.[47]

Feminine character was important because government officials generally viewed women as being responsible for "republican motherhood," in which a woman's duty was to raise her children into proper political citizenship. For example, Frédéric Le Play, a prominent French sociologist at the time, argued that women were the heart of the nation through motherhood and the home (this was one of the reasons why reformers were so interested in the harm in Islamic areas). Le Play stated that "a woman's true function is the government of the home ... the domestic ministry," where she could shape both the family and public life in general.[48] Many reformers believed that women were a type of "angel of the household" and had an innate ability to maintain peace and moral and social standards within the home. This transferred to a sort of "familial feminism" in which these values within the home were the basis in turn for a successful nation to the colonies.[49]

French reformers and colonial officials used domestic science manuals aimed at women who would be setting up households in the colonies to emphasize that French homes were to be warm and welcoming places for everyone who might visit, and that women should focus on such things as cooking and diet, cleanliness and hygiene, child-drearing, and overseeing servants.[50] The idea here was that the colonial Indochinese home should replicate the French metropolitan home as closely as possible. Colonial advice manuals emphasized the need for French furnishings in the colonies (which was ironic, given that Asian furnishing and décor was fashionable in the metropole). Clotilde Chivas-Baron banned Vietnamese décor in her home and advised women to ship French goods (either purchased or heirlooms) from the metropole.[51]

Reformers also focused on diet as a way to maintain cultural Frenchness. For example, an advice article in the "Bulletin of the Colonial Work of French Women" ("Bulletin de l'Oeuvre colonial des femmes français"), a publication aimed at preparing women for life in the colonies, claimed that the French colonial diet should be as close to that of metropole as possible. Foods like cheese, sardines, and olives could

---

47. Nikki Cooper, "(En)gendering Indochina: Feminisation and Female Figurings in French Colonial Discourses," *Women's Studies International Forum* 23, no. 6 (2000): 749–759, 757.

48. Quoted in Horne, "In Pursuit of Greater France," 30.

49. The term "familial feminism" comes from Karen Offen, "Depopulation, Nationalism, and Feminism in Fin-de-Siècle France," *American Historical Review* 89, no. 3 (June 1984): 648–676 Seealso Horne, "In Pursuit of Greater France," 35.

50. Ann Laura Stoler, "Making Empire Respectable: The Politics of Race and Sexual Morality in 20th-Century Colonial Cultures," *American Ethnologist* 16, no. 4 (1989): 648–49.

51. Ha, *French Women & the Empire*, 57–58.

be shipped from France and then supplemented with vegetables from the colonial kitchen garden. These dishes would be cooked and served in items brought from the metropole as well and served by local people in the proper uniforms, including white gloves when serving official dinners.[52] While this type of replication of the metropole may have been the goal of the advice manuals, in reality colonial households were often much more mixed in terms of furnishings and food, as even with steam power, shipping European items to Indochina was often expensive or impossible.

Colonial officials also envisioned Frenchwomen's presence as having a rippling effect beyond the home. With European women came an attempt to remake European settlements to be more like the metropole, because colonial officials viewed women as needing more comfort via European amenities—larger houses, with more space to enclose them from their surroundings, and a larger number of servants.[53] Yet at the same time French women were often criticized for being overly materialistic, and for introducing what some social commenters saw as an artificiality. For example, Louis Roubaud noted in a 1931 work on Indochina that French women used crass displays of goods to gain power, something that he felt was against the colonial spirit that was supposed to unite colonizer and colonized.[54]

In addition to their households, colonial officials generally saw European women serving as a type of cultural ambassador for French values to the colonized population. This was to be done primarily through the instruction of servants within the Frenchwoman's home, and through benevolent works with local communities. In the case of servants, in Indochina officials and the French community in general expected French families to have at least one male or female Vietnamese servant in the household, with duties generally broken down by gender; men served as gardeners, coachmen, houseboys, or cooks, and women as nursemaids. Colonial advice manuals argued that the best way for French women to teach Vietnamese servants was to be an example for them to emulate, particularly in terms of feminine qualities of grace and kindness (although balanced with a firm managerial hand).[55] However, the fact that few Frenchwomen spoke Vietnamese and few Vietnamese servants spoke French often meant that Frenchwomen found it very difficult to get servants to do what they felt was necessary or proper.

Reformers also envisioned French women going to visit women in their own homes, particularly in Algeria. Reformers saw French women as most able to target women in North Africa, especially those who were in harems and secluded. As Georges Vabran told the Musée Social in 1913, "[o]nly the hand of a woman can lift the veil which protects Muslim women."[56] The same reformers

---

52. Ha, *French Women & the Empire*, 58–59, 65.

53. Stoler, "Making Empire Respectable," 640.

54. Cooper, *France in Indochina*, 139.

55. Ha, *French Women & the Empire*, 63, 226.

56. Quoted in Horne, "In Pursuit of Greater France," 38.

who saw the Muslim home as resistant to modernization therefore saw French women as the only ones who could as intermediaries between Muslim women and the larger French culture.[57] The Comtesse Bernard d'Attanoux argued that these Muslim women had a lot of influence within the home, particularly in terms of children's acceptance of French colonial rule. D'Attanoux set up sewing workshops across Algiers-Mustapha in an attempt to teach Algerian women needlework, which she felt would endear French women (and French imperialism) to them.[58]

Sending Frenchwomen to the colonies not only benefitted male colonial officials and colonized people, reformers thought, but it was also seen as a way to reduce the surplus of college-educated single women within the French metropole. Reformers argued that for those who were discontent or quarrelsome, the colonies could serve as a type of safety valve. However, reformers were concerned that the wholesale dumping of these people into the colonies would damage both French prestige and the colonizing effort, and toward the end of the 1800s they began to discuss the idea that "quality" emigrants would be needed.[59] For some reformers, the solution to this was to recruit middle-class women, who could not only provide a "civilizing" influence in the colonies, but would also solve the problem of French women with college educations who didn't have jobs. The Comte d'Haussonville, who was one of the proponents of the emigration of these women to the colonies, argued that since they had already broken female conventions of bourgeois society by getting educations, it would be easier to persuade them to go abroad.[60]

In the late nineteenth and early twentieth centuries, some of these reformers formed emigrant aid societies. The main two of these organizations were the French Society for the Emigration of Women (Société français d'émigration des femmes or SFEF) and the French Colonial Union (Union colonial français or UCF). Both of these were founded in the 1890s and were organized in order to help French women emigrate from the metropole from the colony. While both organizations claimed to promote settler colonization generally, the French Colonial Union was essentially a match-making agency. Through publications, speeches, and fair exhibits, these groups attempted to tell men and women how they could profitably settle in the colonies, and to prepare them for life there.

However, there were also strong class dimensions to the idea that French women would act in appropriately feminine ways. For example, many emigrant aid societies focused on bourgeois/middle-class women rather than working-class women. This was partly because French officials felt it was necessary to maintain a racial

---

57. Horne, "In Pursuit of Greater France," 39.

58. Ha, *French Women & the Empire*, 67–68.

59. Ha, *French Women and the Empire*, 22.

60. Horne, "In Pursuit of Greater France," 36–37.

hierarchy, in which a Frenchwoman was never to work for non-Europeans. As the Comtesse de Custine argued in an advice column, those working in professions such as laundry and tailoring should only work for other French men and women; to do otherwise risked French racial dignity.[61] In general, advice manuals and SFEF and UCF literature tended to view women's work as only a stop-gap measure until the women could find an appropriate colonial French man to marry, at which time they would retire to their households and become full-time wives and mothers.

However, things didn't always work out as colonial officials hoped, for men or women. In Hanoi, one example of someone who violated gender, racial, and class norms was Albert Courcier, who had been convicted of being a vagabond (homeless) and of violence multiple times, from Luxemburg and Metz, in Northern France, and then Hanoi, where he was a manual laborer. In Hanoi in 1908, Courcier claimed that he had been attacked by a Vietnamese woman because he joked to a friend that she was a prostitute. French officials determined that the woman was indeed most likely a prostitute, but the events were very different from Courcier's story. When the unnamed Vietnamese woman had refused to engage Courcier and his friend as clients and tried to shut her door on them, Courcier slapped her, after which she threw a brick at him. The authorities dismissed his case, and even found him guilty of mis-demeanor violence (*violence légéres*). While there was a definite racial aspect to this—Courcier claimed in his defense that as a Frenchman he was superior to the other European railway workers with whom he was employed—there is also a strong gender component.[62] Courcier was not financially stable, he was not married, and he was likely having sex with Vietnamese women (one presumes that this was not the first time he was in the Vietnamese quarter of Hanoi).

Nor would Isabelle Eberhardt have been the kind of woman settler of whom French colonial officials would have approved. Eberhardt and her mother moved to Algeria in 1897, and both converted to Islam. Isabelle also took the male name Si Mahmoud Essadi and began dressing as a man, traveling around North Africa as a travel writer. After her mother died Eberhardt married Slimane Ehnni, a Muslim Algerian of French ethnicity. When she did so, however, she claimed that he should remember that she was not "a vulgar Fatma or any Aïcha" ("une vulgarize Fatma ou une Aïcha quelconque")—stereotypical names for Arabic Muslim women.[63] While Eberhardt was highly critical of the French metropole and the colonial process in general, she reserved some of her harshest criticism for both French and Arab women. Of French women she wrote: "[w]omen can not understand me, they

61. Ha, *French Women & the Empire*, 99.

62. Vann, "White City on the Red River," 517–18.

63. Michelle Chilcoat, "Anticolonialism and Misogyny in the Writings of Isabelle Eberhardt," *The French Review* 77, no. 5 (2004): 949–957, 949.

consider me a strange being. I am much too simple for their taste for the artificial and artifice" ("*Les femmes ne peuvent pas me comprendre, ells me considèrent un être étrange. Je suis beaucoup trop simple pour leur gout épris d'artificiel et d'artifices*").[64] However, in her fictional writing, Arab and Jewish women characters (who were mostly prostitutes) were not cast in a positive light, and often died violently.[65] As historian Michelle Chilcoat explains, Eberhardt seemed to dislike women for their feminine characteristics: "They cannot tolerate solitude, and they always need to know things, like when their lover will be coming back, or what the future holds for them."[66] Despite her critiques of imperialism in general, Eberhardt dealt with the Algerian colonial settlers less harshly, tending to portray them in her fictional works as people who were simply trying to make their way in the world.

While colonial officials viewed Frenchwomen as critical to colonization, their proximity to indigenous men was also cause for concern. This was partly because many indigenous servants were men; in French Indochina the term for a servant was *boy* (regardless of whether the servant was male or female). However, European communities also became focused on European women's safety and sexual racial purity (as sexual partners only for European men) at times of stress within the European communities (this was true of colonies generally, not just French colonies).

For example, when non-European men attempted to push for greater access to education or freedom of movements, European communities would often level charges of attempted rape within the area of a white residence. Rather than being treated as an isolated incident, however, Europeans would extend the "danger" to all non-European men as potential sexual aggressors against white women. This in turn would lead to increased surveillance and control of colonized peoples in the area, with harsh laws focused on even minor (nonsexual) transgressions, and an increased racial segregation. Not only were non-European men targeted in these types of actions, but European women were often also blamed for "provoking" the "hypersexuality" of indigenous men, and so were restricted as well. Ultimately, these types of actions were about European men's respectability and their ability to provide and protect their families.[67]

Conclusion

We began this chapter by examining Delacroix's *The Women of Algiers* as an image of women in Orientalist discourse, and we followed those ideas through different spaces of imperialism within French Algeria and Indochina. Before we leave this

---

64. Quoted in Chilcoat, "Anticolonialism and Misogyny," 950.

65. Chilcoat, "Anticolonialism and Misogyny," 952.

66. Chilcoat, "Anticolonialism and Misogyny," 953.

67. Stoler, "Making Empire Respectable," 641–42.

topic, however, we need to remember that the realities of life on the ground in Algeria and Indochina were rarely so straightforward as colonial officials would have liked. Algerian and Vietnamese men and women, and European men and women, often failed to completely adhere to the stereotypes bestowed upon them. Men and women crossed races to form lasting bonds with each other. As we saw from Albert Courcier and Isabelle Eberhardt, European men and women did not always conform to ideas of a head-of-household benevolent father or a homemaking Christian mother. People within the colonies rarely fell into neat categories. For example, in Algeria there was a large population of people from Mediterranean countries besides France, and a substantial Jewish population. As we saw in the case of the Wallachian women in Hanoi, in addition to Chinese, Japanese, and Korean people in Indochina there were non-French Europeans, as well as people from other French colonies (particularly the French colony in India, Pondicherry).

Over the course of the mid-nineteenth and early twentieth centuries, French imperialism shifted from the idea of assimilation, in which officials attempted to make colonial people part of the nation without distinction from metropolitan citizens (an effort that was both unsuccessful and problematic), to the idea of association, in which colonies could be held in a type of confederacy with the metropole, without being synonymous with it. In other words, colonization went from being a single French state, unified across vast geographic distances, to a group of entities that made up a larger whole (in this case, Greater France). France was far from alone in both simultaneously extending and dividing colonial identity and citizenship. As we will see in the next chapter, which focuses on British India and Egypt, gender played a significant role in nationalist movements in the late nineteenth and early twentieth centuries as well.

FURTHER READING

Booth, Marilyn, ed. *Harem Histories: Envisioning Places and Living Spaces.* Durham, NC: Duke University Press, 2010.

Çelik, Zeynep. *Urban Forms and Colonial Confrontations: Algiers under French Rule.* Berkeley: University of California Press, 1997.

Ha, Marie-Paule. *French Women and the Empire: The Case of Indochina.* Oxford: Oxford University Press, 2014.

Isom-Verhaaren, Christine. "Royal French Women in the Ottoman Sultans' Harem: The Political Uses of Fabricated Accounts from the Sixteenth to the Twenty-First Century." *Journal of World History* 17, no. 2 (June 2006): 159–96.

Sessions, Jennifer E. *By Sword and Plow: France and the Conquest of Algeria.* Ithaca, NY: Cornell University Press, 2011.

Vann, Michael G. "Sex and the Colonial City: Mapping Masculinity, Whiteness, and Desire in French Occupied Hanoi." *Journal of World History* 28, no. 3–4 (December 2017): 395–435.

4 GENDER, ATTIRE, AND NATIONALIST MOVEMENTS IN INDIA AND EGYPT

In his autobiography, Mohandas K. Gandhi recounted his child-hood, his time studying at university in England, his work in South Africa, and his return to India after many years away. At the end of his life story, however, he turned to a subject that will likely sound strange to you: cloth. Over the course of two chapters, titled "The Birth of *Khadi*" and "Found at Last!" Gandhi described his search for people who could acquire raw cotton fiber, turn it into thread using a tradi-tional Indian spinning wheel, and weave it into a rough traditional cloth referred to as *khadi*.

Why the fuss over cloth? All the fabric in the clothes that you are wearing has very likely been produced by machine—spinning the fiber into yarn, and then weaving or knitting that yarn into cloth. This has essentially been the case since the early nineteenth century, when cloth from textile mills, which could produce fabric at a fraction of the cost of handmade cloth, started to dominate the world market.[1]

The industrialization of textile production caused a great amount of social change, and the fact that handmade cloth had essentially disappeared by the early twentieth century was precisely Gandhi's point. Until the 1750s, India produced one-fourth of the world's manufactured goods, much of it hand-produced cotton cloth. You may remember from chapter 2 that Indian calico was important in the transatlantic economy, as European traders used it and other goods to purchase slaves from West Africa. Ironically, some of these same enslaved people began to grow cotton in the American South, which then found its way to England, where it fueled an explosion in cloth production and the building of textile mills there (as well as back in the United States).

Cotton cloth was at the center of the British imperial economy. In the early 1800s, England made huge quantities of cloth for export. And since they controlled most of India through the British East India Company, the government placed tariffs as high as 78 percent

---

1. See Bernard S. Cohn, *Colonialism and its Forms of Knowledge: The British in India* (Princeton, NJ: Princeton University Press, 1996), especially the chapter "Cloth, Clothes, and Colonialism."

on South Asian cloth so that it would not compete with their more expensive British-produced product. When the Union Navy cut off exports of slave-grown cotton from the Confederacy during the US Civil War, Britain had to rapidly switch sources for cotton, and invested heavily in *growing* of cotton fiber in India but kept the *processing* of yarn and cloth in their own cotton mills. The result of these policies was that over the course of the nineteenth century , Britain essentially destroyed India's cotton industry.

Gandhi therefore focused on cloth as a symbol not only of capitalism, which created massive economic inequalities across the globe, but also as a specific symbol of the exploitation of British colonialism that had robbed India of its wealth. He argued that in order to attain *swaraj* (home rule or independence), India needed to engage in *swadeshi* (loosely translated as "own country"), becoming economically self-sufficient through the purchase of Indian-made goods. No more would British manufacturers sell British-made cloth, tailored to Indian tastes, in India. Instead, Gandhi argued that Indians had to learn to spin using a traditional type of spinning wheel called a *charkha* and weave their own cloth the khadi that people had worn in one form of another for centuries. Khadi therefore became a potent symbol of India's independence movement, so much so that the charkha appears on the flag of India even today.

Gandhi's emphasis on the wearing of Indian cloth was also closely linked to the role of the body and its meanings within nationalist anticolonial movements, because imperial governments gendered the colonized body—both male and female. Imperialism worked under a number of basic assumptions about the body and its relation to "civilization" (you may remember one example of this—neurasthenia—which we explored in chapter 3). Europeans saw their civilizations as more "masculine," and therefore more rational and logical in how they governed.

At the same time, Europeans portrayed colonized people as more "effeminate" and less logical. In fact, the terms "effeminate" and "emasculated" were often used by British officials in Africa, India, and East Asia. Closely related to this was the idea that Europeans were more civilized and, in theory, should rule these foreign territories until those populations were on the same level as the colonizing power.

These ideas of civilization carried into how colonial officials viewed the body. We tend to think of our bodies as not being tied to any political context or meaning, but human bodies were and are seen and acted upon in ways that reflect struggles for power. Both colonial officials and the nationalists who challenged their rule tied the fate of the nation to the physical prowess and fertility of its citizens. Those who had power and wanted to preserve it, for example, focused their arguments on the "gender" of the colonized.

We see this in the way that colonial officials generally assigned feminine characteristics to colonized men, particularly men in India. British politicians, in arguing that women in general were biologically inferior and mentally incapable of voting responsibly, applied the same ideas in India: the country could never be independent because men like Gandhi were made too effeminate by the effects of a hot climate and centuries of racial impurity. This gendered ideology was partly an outgrowth of the types of eugenic arguments common in the mid- to late 1800s and early 1900s (as we saw in chapter 3), The big question that loomed behind all of these inter-sections of gender, race, and nation, ultimately turned on who had full rights as citizens—whose body could be called for military service, exercise citizenship rights such as voting, and be in governmental spaces. Gandhi was well aware of this.

In their work within independence movements, nationalists had to create (or re-create) a national identity. Although it may seem strange to us, because we are used to thinking of ourselves as citizens of a nation, nations are in fact artificial creations—they group people together based on a series of criteria, such as an imagined common past, an ethnic identity, language, and so on.[2] Scholars have long debated what ties citizens together,—what makes them willing to fight and die for people they have never met, or to embrace an abstract concept like the "British way of life." Perhaps the most influential of these intellectuals is Benedict Anderson, who theorized in his book *Imagined Communities* that nations were created through "print capitalism." This was fundamentally about newspapers, published in a common language that regular people could understand (rather than something more elite, like Latin), and that gave people knowledge about a series of events of national importance (in essence, a shared experience to discuss with one another).[3]

Even though Anderson included colonies in his analysis, some scholars of imperialism have raised questions about his theories and the limits of national-ism. For example, what about people who were living within nations but didn't have full citizenship rights, such as African-origin peoples and women? What were the differences between a "subject" and a "citizen"—could Indian people, for example, be subjects of the British crown without enjoying many of the rights of citizens? How could nationalist movements grow in places where most of the population couldn't read (particularly before radio)? Our focus on the body in this chapter puts us in dialogue with these questions.

For our case studies in this chapter, I have chosen India and Egypt because they are similar in some ways, even though they are geographically far apart (see the map in 4.1). India was a formal British colony starting in 1858, when the British government took it over from the British East India Company (EIC). The EIC had governed some parts of India directly and others through proxy rulers. In Egypt, the British took control in 1882 in the wake of a finan-cial collapse and an uprising by Egyptian nationalists led by Ahmed 'Urabi.

---

2. See Jesse Spohnholz, *Ruptured Lives: Refugee Crises in Historical Perspective* (New York: Oxford University Press, 2020).

3. Benedict Anderson, *Imagined Communities: Reflections on the Origin and Spread of Nationalism* (London: Verso, 1998).

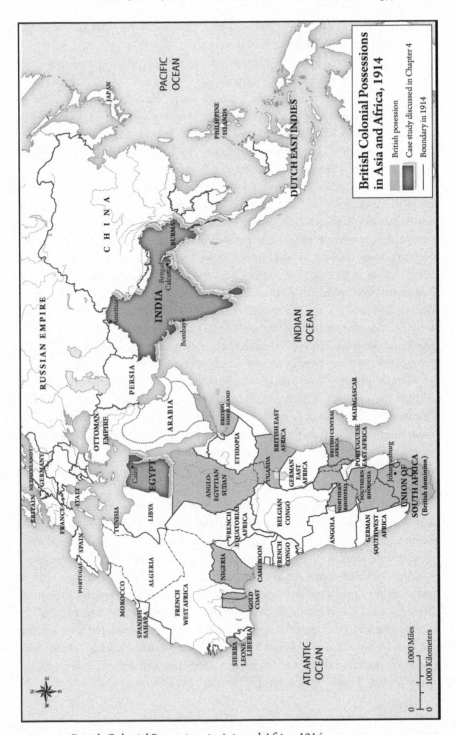

MAP 4.1 British Colonial Possessions in Asia and Africa, 1914

Although they left the Khedive, or viceroy, as the face of the government, British colonial officials essentially ran the country.

In the wake of World War I, both Indians and Egyptians staged nationalist uprisings that the British government violently repressed. The Jallianwala Bagh (Amritsar) massacre in India, when troops under British command killed or wounded over 1,600 people, was one such case of repression. In 1919 (the same year as Jallianwala Bagh), Egyptians engaged in a pro-independence revolution. Despite the passage of a new Egyptian constitution in 1924, Britain did not formally leave the country until 1954, and India did not gain independence until 1947.

Both areas were also relatively complex in terms of nationalism. As a colony, India was a combination of many different princely states, some of which retained a degree of local autonomy, while others did not. Egypt had officially been part of the Ottoman Empire until it was dismantled in the wake of World War I. Nationalist movements in both areas struggled to build a sense of coherence and allegiance to something that was new, rather than to an administrative state that had existed before British control. In other words, Egyptian nationalists had to build a *separate* identity that was distinctly *Egyptian* rather than *Ottoman*, and Indian nationalists had to build *unified Indian* identity rather than allegiance to a particular province, many of which had their own language and cultural distinctions. As we will see, these efforts were only partly successful.

Gender played a key role in these movements in that nationalists had to address the types of civilizational ideas that Britain deployed to justify their continued presence and control. Gender was also directly related to ideas of modernity—that Indian/Egyptian men and women needed to become modern in order to be capable of self-rule. The question for nationalists was the kind of modernity they would adopt—one that had essentially the same aspects as the West, or one that would be distinctly Indian/Egyptian.

One of the common ways that nationalists of all types (not just those struggling against imperialism) used gender was by creating binaries, with firm gender roles where men were physically strong, militarily capable, and politically rational while women were weak, in need of protection, and domestically focused. This type of masculinity, which some scholars have termed "muscular nationalism," prized physical strength; a man should be armed and ready to kill and sacrifice for the nation. In contrast to this, women were to be "mothers of the nation," nonviolent and domestic, who served as figures to be protected by men.[4] As we will see, however, this binary tended to be more fraught in real life, most particularly when women were physically present and involved in protest and politics, and as they became political actors and used their physical presence to assert their own agendas.

---

4. Sikata Banerjee, *Muscular Nationalism: Gender, Violence, and Empire in India and Ireland, 1914–2004* (New York: New York University Press, 2014).

The Body Itself

As we saw in chapter 3, the bodies of colonial women played a crucial role in imperialism. The idea that Oriental women were downtrodden or oppressed was a stock defense for European colonization of North Africa and Asia. When we look at the case of Indian women, we see the ways that Indian men, and British men and women, all used the debate over women's bodies for their own political ends.

Women's bodies were the focus of debates about several cultural practices. In India there were three major reform movements having to do with women's lives and sexuality. First, there was the anti–*sati* movement in the early and mid-1800s, where British missionaries stoked the ire of the British public against what missionaries saw as the widespread practice of sati or widow immolation, where widows would throw themselves upon their husband's funeral pyres. Although this practice was limited to specific geographic areas of India and upper castes, the British press portrayed it as much more widespread and it became a stereotype for the supposedly barbaric practices of Hindus.

The debate in India and Britain about sati intensified in 1813, when the East India Company legalized the practice, but on the condition that the widow had to voluntarily throw herself on the pyre. This sparked an intense discussion among British missionaries and social reformers, Orthodox Hindus, and Indian reformers. The disputes centered around the origins of sati (whether it was an authentic practice from the Hindu Vedas, or a misunderstanding of them), and whether the women's actions could be counted as truly voluntary or whether the women were coerced by family members. In these deliberations, however, the sources that we have are from British and Indian men—few asked women themselves what they thought or felt. Some British authors claimed to have asked women if they were voluntarily going to the pyre, but tended to not believe the women if they answered in the affirmative.

In the second and third major reform movements, the Age of Consent Act in the 1880s and 1890s and the Child Marriage Restraint Act (or Sarda Act) in 1929, Indian women themselves took a more active role. Here, the issue was the age at which women and girls could consent to sex. Child marriage (which I will define here as those under the age of fourteen) was a relatively common practice in India, however, the marriage was not supposed to be consummated until the girl had her first menstruation. One of the major changes between the sati and the Age of Consent Act debates was that while the former had been largely limited to elites, discussions about the latter galvanized broader public opinion, as Indian leaders tried to connect nationalist politics and reform.

One event that shows the complexity of reforming the age of consent was the legal case of Rukhmabai, who sued for divorce in the British colonial courts. Rukhmabai was married to Dadaji Bhikaji when she was eleven and he was twenty. However, when Rukhmabai reached puberty, she refused to move into Bhikaji's home—a decision her stepfather supported. In 1884 Bhikaji sued for his conjugal rights, and the case moved up the courts to the Bombay High Court, where Justice Charles Farran ruled that Rukhmabai had to either go live with her husband or face six months in prison. Rukhmabai chose prison.[5]

Rukhmabai did not quietly fade away, but rather responded to Farran's decision by publishing several letters in the *Times of India* in 1885 under the name "The Hindu Lady," outlining her case against child marriage and enforced widowhood. These caused intense debate in the press and women's publications. Rukhmabai argued that child marriage destroyed women's lives because it put girls into a hierarchical setting in their in-law's homes, where girls were socialized into being passive and docile.

Rukhmabai's argument went against the rationale of rights that some Indian nationalist men espoused. Although nationalist men had also wanted to reform child marriage customs, their arguments tended to be based on eugenics—that child marriage led to young mothers, which was bad for Indians as a race. Other men asserted that it was the women themselves who advocated child marriage because they wanted to enjoy the pomp and circumstance that came with the ceremonies.[6] Instead, Rukhmabai made her case based on women's rights: that child marriage should be abolished because the girls themselves needed time to develop intellectually. While Rukhmabai's case spurred debate about the issue of consent, it was the death of eleven-year-old Phulmoni Dasi, who was raped by her thirty-five-year-old husband, that was the immediate catalyst for passing the Age of Consent Act.

At the heart of both sati and the Age of Consent Act was also the idea of who was civilized and who was not. In both of these debates, the EIC and British colonial government had to balance pressure to end these practices (which largely came from some segments of the British public) with the practicalities of managing India, where they could not afford to alienate elite Indians who cooperated with the British colonial state. In practicality, while the colonial government might pass laws and restrict practices, officials were also very attuned to resistance from orthodox Hindus who argued that the British government should butt out of legislating fundamental Hindu religious practices. Indeed, the British had forcefully learned this lesson when their disregard of Hindu and Muslim cultural norms sparked revolution in 1857.

5. Padma Anagol, "Rebellious Wives and Dysfunctional Marriages: Indian Women's Discourses and Participation in the Debates over Restitution of Conjugal Rights and the Child Marriage Controversy in the 1800s and 1890s," in *Women and Social Reform in Modern India: A Reader*, ed. Sumit Sarkar and Tanika Sarkar (Bloomington: University of Indiana Press, 2008), 282-312; 292–293

6. Anagol, "Rebellious Wives and Dysfunctional Marriages," 294–96.

We see this care for Hindu traditions in the Rukhmabai case. Judge Farran—who was Irish—deviated from British Christian laws, which would not have forced a woman to go to her husband's home if the marriage hadn't been consummated. Instead, Farran relied upon orthodox Hindu opinions, in which a girl-bride belonged to her husband and his household, whether she was physically located in her natal family's house or not.[7] In essence, he took the opinion of orthodox Hindu men as his guidance in the case, giving them reason to support the British colonial government rather than resist it.

By the 1930s both nationalist and women's movements were well-established in India, and Indian women were more directly involved with debates about the Sarda Act, or Child Marriage Restraint Act of 1929. The act outlawed marriages for boys younger than sixteen and girls younger than fourteen (although it would take ten years of modification to be able to enforce the law). For our purposes, this act is important for several reasons. One was that Indian nationalist women took an active part in the debates over the act. While nationalist men's groups in the 1920s had fractured into subgroups based around gender, class, sectarian politics, or caste, women's groups had maintained broader unity, especially the All-Indian Women's Association.[8]

Second, nationalist women used the debates over the bill to flip the argument about who was "civilized" and who was "savage." We see this in their response to Katherine Mayo, an American pro-imperialist who wrote an expose titled *Mother India*, in which she argued that Hinduism encouraged sexual excess of men and women, and that this was the root cause of Indian "degeneracy." Mayo asserted that British rule was therefore the only way to civilize and modernize Indians.[9] Nationalist women contended that while there were indeed outdated social traditions, reform movements that would change them should come from nationalists and not from the British government. They further argued that the colonial government was ineffective at reform and had not done *enough* to protect women—as was evidenced by cases such as Rukhmabai's. In other words, nationalist women flipped the script and asserted that *they* were the force for modernization, not the British colonial government.[10]

In campaigning for the Sarda Act, nationalist women also physically moved into the public sphere. This signaled a sea change from earlier anticolonial movements in which women were supposed to be the carriers of tradition by remaining out of the public and politics. In 1928, for example, the most important feminist

7. Anagol, "Rebellious Wives and Dysfunctional Marriages," 292–293.

8. Mrinalini Sinha, "The Lineage of the 'Indian' Modern: Rhetoric, Agency, and the Sarda Act," in *Gender, Sexuality and Colonial Modernities*, ed. Antoinette Burton (London: Routledge, 1999), 209–224, 210.

9. Sinha, "The Lineage of the 'Indian' Modern," 210–211.

10. Sinha, "The Lineage of the 'Indian' Modern," 213.

journal in India, the *Stri Dharma*, argued that women had to become involved in politics because "social reform and politics are not only interdependent but also because as long as we need to arm ourselves with legislative enactment for social reconstruction, it means that we depend upon political instruments for our purpose." Women from organizations like the All-India Women's Conference (AIWC) began turning up at nationalist politician's offices and telling them what the AIWC wanted. They not only kept pressure on pro-Sarda Act politicians to continue to support the act, they also protested opponents of the bill so forcefully that some male politicians complained about harassment.[11] In embarking on this very public activism, nationalist women incorporated themselves as voices and agents within the nationalist movement itself.

In Egypt, women focused on the reform of polygamy and the household structure in general. Under Ottoman rule, Egypt had maintained a system of domestic slavery in which women (largely from Ethiopia and Sudan) were bought for household labor. This was a widespread enough practice that even peasant families bought occasionally bought household slaves. However, the Anglo-Egyptian Convention in 1877 (after which Britain essentially occupied Egypt), outlawed the slave trade and ordered that slaves be manumitted.

At the same time, the economy itself changed when the British forced more farmers to plant cotton and introduced wage work in factories. Egyptian feminists used the Anglo-Egyptian Convention and economic changes to push for changes within the home, where men were the primary wage earners and women became household managers. They also sought to define the household more narrowly to the nuclear family and pushed for "companionate marriage" (the idea that husband and wife would be friends) and monogamy.

Some Egyptian women condemned arranged marriages, as well as child marriage, which (as it did in India) tended to lead to wide age gaps between husband and wife. For example, in 1911 the newspaper *Al-'Afaf* ran a story of a twenty-year-old educated woman who was forced to marry a wealthy eighty-year-old man, after which she attempted suicide. The editor argued that this was an example of the gross injustice of arranged marriage.[12] In a series of letters published in *al-Jarida*, Egyptian feminists Malak Hifni Nassef and Mai Ziyada discussed marital reforms. Nassef asserted that educational rights and marriage reform should be the main focus of Egyptian women. Instead of what they deemed "superficial" reformtopics such as whether or not women should wear veils, Nassef took aim at polygamy, which was "laden with savagery and selfishness" because it caused pain and suffering to the first wife and the children of that union.[13]

---

11. Sinha, "The Lineage of the 'Indian' Modern," 214–15.

12. Beth Baron, *The Women's Awakening in Egypt: Culture, Society, and the Press* (New Haven, CT: Yale University Press, 1994), 165.

13. Ahmed, *Women and Gender in Islam*, 181–82.

Gender and imperialism played a role in how nationalists viewed male bodies as well as female. As we saw in the previous chapter, at the end of the nineteenth century many colonial officials became concerned about the physical bodies of colonizers. Neurasthenia, or "overcivilization," seemed to be rampant in European colonial officials, a diagnosis that required these men to have rest cures in places like Dalat in Indochina. However, some colonized men also took up the idea that their societies had once been strong, but their physical strength had faded, allowing colonial domination. The way back to independence was therefore to increase their individual physical strength. Some nationalists in India, for example, sponsored athletic events and a significant number of them advocated eating a more European diet as a way to grow physically stronger. Even the vegetarian Gandhi confessed that he secretly tried meat in the belief that it might generate muscle growth.

Some nationalist men in Egypt and India focused on ideas of "muscular nationalism" that were also present in many nations in the early twentieth century. This was when the modern summer Olympics emerged, and the popularity of bodybuilding spread to everyday people instead of being reserved for the circus strongman. Muscular nationalism was partly as a reaction to European imperialists who had intertwined ideas of physical prowess, race, and nationality as a justification for conquering other people. Colonial officials also used muscular nationalism as a tool to divide groups against one another—for example the British portrayed Gurkhas and Marathas in India as "natural warriors" while denigrating Bengali men as weak and effeminate. Added to this was the eugenics movement's emphasis on physical fitness, in which racially superior people were both mentally and physically strong.

However, in India, the connections between physical prowess and masculinity was present before the twentieth century. For example, Nagendra Prasad Sarbadhikari used the example of physical fitness in Europe to advocate for muscular nationalism. One story he told recounted an incident in which a group of clerks were making fun of him for his muscles. Sarbadhikari lifted one of the men off the ground and said, "those who speak like this—they are the ones who are afraid to step out on the streets with their wives and daughters; and when they do [they] are unable to safeguard their honour."[14] As we see here, the ability to protect (supposedly) weak women was a key part of Sarbadhikari's construction of masculinity, and the need for men's physical strength. It is also no coincidence that the villains in Sarbadhikari's tale were clerks—Bengali commentators and satirists had created the term "babu" to refer to Indian men who were low-level civil servants, lawyers, or publishers. The babus were targeted for ridicule from both sides—by Indians who saw them as caving to British and Western norms,

---

14. Sikata Banerjee, *Muscular Nationalism: Gender, Violence, and Empire in India and Ireland, 1914–2004* (New York: New York University Press, 2012), 55.

and by colonial officials who saw them as effeminate, physically weak, and untrustworthy.[15]

Some Indian nationalists drew upon the idea of a Hindu warrior image for masculine ideals, such as religious leader Swami Vivekananda. Vivekananda's *kshatra-virya* (warrior strength) incorporated physical strength and decisiveness; men did not hesitate to use force when threatened. Vivekananda asserted that "through centuries of slavery, we have become like a nation of women"— quarreling, and criticizing other Indian men for wanting to lead while accepting abuse from British men. Instead he advocated physical force, and criticized those who looked to nonviolence, like Gandhi, as effeminate. There was also an element of asceticism, connecting the idea to the Hindu *sannyasi* or monk who bore hardships, made sacrifices, and engaged in spiritual penance. This allowed muscular nationalists to test their strength through spirituality rather than martial means.[16]

For women, Vivekananda envisioned a much more circumscribed role. While some women could take part in public and violent acts, he asserted that the roles of wife and mother were the most appropriate and laudable for women. Vivekananda wrote that "the height of a woman's ambition is to be like Sita . . . the patient, the all-suffering, the ever-faithful, the ever-pure wife." In other words, "the ideal woman . . . is the mother, the mother first, and the mother last."[17] In this he didn't see any particular need for reform among Indian women.

While in India those who advocated for muscular nationalism tended to be more elite, in Egypt it was the effendi—the clerks themselves who subscribed to the idea. Popular periodicals such as *al-Muqtataf* and *Al-Hilal* promoted exercise and physical fitness in schools in order to build the body of the nation by developing the physical bodies of its subjects. As in India, nationalists in Egypt partly blamed colonization on the decline of the Egyptian male body and asserted that building up men's bodies would therefore aid in anticolonial struggle. However, *al-Muqtataf* also advised women to be physically fit, although the authors of articles tended to base their rationale on more traditional themes like women's physical ability to take care of home and children, and to maintain their physical attractiveness to their husbands.[18]

Egyptian nationalists also saw sports as developing a sense of group solidarity, such as in the National Club for Physical Culture in Cairo, created by several notable Egyptian men in 1909. As ʿAbd al-Khāliq Tharwat (who later became Prime Minister of Egypt) explained in 1919, the sporting club addressed two

---

15. Robert McLain, *Gender and Violence in British India: The Road to Amritsar, 1914–1919* (New York: Palgrave Macmillan, 2014), 9.

16. Banerjee, *Muscular Nationalism*, 58–59.

17. Banerjee, *Muscular Nationalism*, 62.

18. Wilson Chacko Jacob, *Working Out Egypt: Effendi Masculinity and Subject Formation in Colonial Modernity, 1870–1940* (Durham, NC: Duke University Press, 2011), 79.

issues that nationalists identified as problems: the lack of community in elite young men after they left school, and the lack of physical activity.[19]

Nationalists could also use international sporting events to establish an identity, including the Olympic Games. Egyptian nationalist men formed the Egyptian Olympic Committee in 1914, and sent an Egyptian team to the 1920 Olympics in Antwerp and to Paris in 1924. Throughout the 1920s authors in Egyptian publications consistently argued that sports were both a sign of Egyptian progress, and that athletes themselves directly represented the Egyptian nation—the image of the nation and the image of the athlete were in essence one.

The culmination of this idea was the 1928 Olympics in Amsterdam, in which wrestler Ibrahim Mustafa won a gold medal—the first for someone representing an African country. In response promoters launched several sports magazines, including a supplement to *Al-Nil al-Musawwar*, titled *Al-Abtal* (*Champions*). The first supplement appeared in 1932 and included a two-page biography of Mustafa's life and rise to fame, which the author used to mirror the Egyptian nation. Born of humble peasant origins, Mustafa had "visions of strength" in his childhood, learned about sports by watching international weightlifters compete, and started a temporary sports club with his friends called Al-Nadi al-Ahli al-Iskandari, or the Alexandria National Club.

Trained by a coach at an Italian sports club, Mustafa quickly became successful, and went to the 1924 Olympics in Paris. However, he was foiled by his clothing—shoes not meant for wrestling caused him to slip in the ring, and a flimsy uniform that tore easily preoccupied him as he tried to hold the pieces together. After this humiliating defeat, Mustafa returned to Egypt and was forced to spend all his time working to earn a living. Taken again under the wing of his trainer at the Italian club, Mustafa qualified for the Amsterdam games again in 1928 and this time (with the proper equipment) brought home gold, returning to a job with the government and training aspiring wrestlers.[20]

Mustafa's biography in *Al-Abtal* connected with some of the broader nationalist origin stories for Egypt. From humble, peasant backgrounds, Egyptians learned from others in the Mediterranean, adopting new methods and technologies while maintaining their roots. When competing on the international stage against other nations, Egyptians were deliberately handicapped by Europeans, given insufficient tools to be successful. However, as the author of the biography argued, Egypt did not remain defeated. Instead it emerged from hardship physically stronger, this time with the right tools to defeat all other nations.

As these examples illustrate, men's and women's bodies were an important part of Indian and Egyptian nationalist identity and movements. Men and women nationalists used the body—what it looked like, who it had sex with and

19. Jacob, *Working Out Egypt*, 87.

20. Jacob, *Working Out Egypt*, 142–44.

when—in order to create larger arguments about the nation. A key aspect of this was nationalist connections to modernity. For women, nationalist modernity meant that they should be more than just their reproductive capacities, that to be a modern Egyptian or Indian woman was to be in a monogamous companionate marriage in which women were able to exercise their intellectual abilities. In short, femininity could be expressed by being involved in intellectual pursuits, including politics. For at least some Egyptian and Indian nationalist men, masculinity was a martial, physically based affair in which strong men embodied a strong nation and vice versa.

Covering the Body: Clothing

Nationalists didn't just connect the body itself to the idea of the nation; they also used clothing. In fact, Indian nationalists mapped onto a long practice of East India Company (EIC) and British colonial officials who consciously used clothing as a marker of their difference from Indians. Most British people maintained their multilayered clothing even when it would have made them physically uncomfortable because the climate in India was so much warmer than in Britain (although some did change fabrics, from wool to linen and cotton). The exception to this was in the Mughal court, where European men tended to wear Indian fashions at home and British dress at official functions. Over time, however, officials began cracking down on these lapses in visual Britishness, and by the mid-1800s the EIC had passed regulations banning British officials from deviating from British dress.[21]

As had been the case with the body, European racialized ideas of civilized versus savage became partly affixed to dress—authors in literature and advice manuals consistently portrayed "savages" as naked or immodestly clothed, while "civilized" people dressed like Europeans. For example, in a 1873 story in the satirical journal *The Indian Charivarti*, one of the characters warned his son about degenerating into Indian dress, stating that "an English gentleman should *always* be dressed, so that, were he suddenly dropped into Bond Street [in London], he would pass *unnoticed* in the crowd."[22] Indeed, in the 1920s, rather than segregating public toilets based on race (and thus instituting the types of racial categories common elsewhere in the British Empire), Calcutta men's toilets were segregated by clothing: "Europeans Only" became "Gentlemen in European Dress." Most British people saw Indian men's dress, which generally consisted of a single length of cloth wrapped around the body, as effeminate. EIC lieutenant-colonial John

---

21. Bernard Cohn, "Cloth, Clothes, and Colonialism: India in the Nineteenth Century," in *Cloth and Human Experience*, ed. Annette B. Weiner and Jane Schneider (Washington, DC: Smithsonian Institution Press, 1989), 303–304, 309–310.

22. Emma Tarlo, *Clothing Matters: Dress and Identity in India* (Chicago: University of Chicago Press, 1996), 37.

Briggs noted in an 1828 letter that Indian elite were clothed "in long flowing linen robes, giving them in our eyes, an air of effeminacy."[23]

Indian men had various reactions to these ideas of clothing as civilization. Some adopted English dress, even though that could lead to other changes in behavior. For example, laces and buckles on English footwear meant that one could not easily remove shoes when going into a house (as was the custom). Suits limited one's ability to sit on the ground, and therefore required additional furniture. Few Indian women adopted European women's dress, so it created a visual gulf between men and women of the same family. And finally, Indian men who adopted complete European dress tended to be condemned by the British as "meaningless imitators" who were only taking on the appearance of civilization, without being truly civilized.[24]

One of those who adopted European-style clothing for part of his life was Gandhi. During his childhood and adolescence, he associated European dress with a conversion to Christianity, and generally disdained it. However, when he traveled to London to study 1888, he took a suitcase full of English clothes. His attempts to blend in immediately failed, however, because when he stepped off the ship in September, he was wearing a white flannel suit that was then out of season (fashionable British people only wore white in the summer). When he returned to India in 1891 he maintained European dress, and encouraged his family to also wear Western clothing.[25] We see this in Figure 4.1, a photograph taken in a studio in Johannesburg, South Africa in 1906, in which Gandhi is dressed in a Western-style suit and appears both confident and relaxed as he leans slightly on a table or basket.

As he spent more time in South Africa in the early 1900s, Gandhi's attitude about clothing changed. As British colonies, people could migrate between them and there was a large population of Indians in South Africa by the end of the 1800s. Many of these people were indentured laborers whose passage was paid by labor bosses in exchange for a set period of work. They faced a lot of discrimination and abuse from both bosses and government officials, and Gandhi became involved in the growing rights movement for Indians in South Africa. As he did so, Gandhi changed his attitude about clothing as well as the clothing itself. He began to adopt provocative clothing by increasingly simplifying his clothes, having them made in plain and coarse cloth (including Australian flour sacks).[26]

Frequently, instead of adopting English dress wholesale, Indian men would do a kind of hybrid, either in Indian styles created from English-made cloth or by mixing European- and Indian-style garments. This could be adopting a European-style suit jacket and shirt, while having Indian clothing below the waist

---

23. Tarlo, *Clothing Matters*, 55; 34.

24. Tarlo, *Clothing Matters*, 24; 45.

25. Tarlo, *Clothing Matters*, 65–66.

26. Tarlo, *Clothing Matters*, 68.

FIGURE 4.1 Gandhi as a lawyer in Johannesburg, South Africa, 1906.
Source: Dinodia Photos / Alamy Stock Photo

(often a *dhoti*, a length of cloth which is wrapped around the waist and legs), or it could be an Indian-style coat with European trousers and shoes. This type of hybrid dressing was particularly common with local elites in rural areas, who could afford the cloth and tailoring that European garments required but who also needed to maintain continuity with local customs. Other Indian men went back and forth between European and Indian-style dress, changing at home, at the office, or somewhere between.

Even before Gandhi, Indian nationalists recognized the potential of clothing. For example, in the late 1800s and early 1900s, nationalists in Bengal (the area in the east of British India) focused on a variety of issues, one of which was clothing. Jyotirindranath Tagore (the elder brother of the poet Rabindranath Tagore) tried to develop a type of national dress that all Indians could wear as a sign of nationalism. However, according to Rabindranath, who was a teenager at the time, the solution that Jyotirindranath came up with was hideously ugly. Rabindranath stated that "there may be many a brave Indian ready to die for his country, but there are but few, I am sure, who even for the good of the nation, would face the public streets in such pan-Indian garb."[27] Needless to say, it did not catch on. Rabindranath himself later tried to develop a national outfit but it also failed to catch on, and in the midst of the Bengali nationalist movement in 1905 (culminating in the partition of Bengal from the rest of British India that year), the dhoti came to symbolize resistance to the British.

As it turned out, Gandhi's attempt to connect nationalist movements to clothing was more successful than the Tagores. He may have left South Africa in British clothing, but by the time he and his wife, Kasturba, arrived in Bombay in 1915, Gandhi had adopted the dress of an Indian peasant from the region of Kathiawadi, as we see in Figure 4.2. In the photo, Gandhi and Kasturba stand in a portrait studio (as Gandhi had for the photo in South Africa in Figure 4.1), and the photo shows the clothing on their entire bodies, including Gandhi's turban and their bare feet. By dressing as an Indian, Gandhi was self-consciously rejecting Western clothing, and by dressing as an Indian *peasant* he was also rejecting the fashion of elite Indian men, with their adoption or blending of fashions.

However, like Jyotirindranath and Rabindranath Tagore, Gandhi realized that regional dress could not be extended into national clothing, and began to try different styles. At the root of these fashion choices, however, was khadi—as we saw at the start of this chapter—and the need for swadeshi. For Gandhi, home-produced cloth was more important than the style of dress, and in the early 1920s he began to wear only a loincloth, in recognition that many of the very poor could not afford enough khadi (which was more expensive than the industrially produced cloth at the time) to make a dhoti. Gandhi had been hesitant to wear only the loincloth, because it could potentially be perceived by British and his fellow Indians as impolite, and as a sign of insanity and extremism. Indeed, he was criticized by some on those accounts.[28] Initially, he stated that he was only going to wear the loincloth for five weeks, until October 1921, which was his deadline for swaraj (home rule or independence). However, when swaraj did not occur, he continued to wear the loincloth as a symbol of the need for swadeshi.

In fact, Gandhi wore only the loincloth and shawl for the rest of his life. That he even dressed only in these two items on a visit to London in 1931, where he met with King George V, shows that the symbols of masculine nationalist

---

27. Tarlo, *Clothing Matters*, 59.

28. Tarlo, *Clothing Matters*, 72.

FIGURE 4.2 Mahatma Gandhi with his wife Kasturba on their return to India from South Africa in 1915.
Source: Mahatma Gandhi with his wife Kasturba on their return to India from South Africa in 1915/ Wikipedia

clothing had come full circle. Initially, to be a civilized man capable of governing one's own nation required Western-style suits, as Gandhi had worn in the late 1800s. However, by the 1920s and 1930s, nationalist clothing for men had literally taken on a different appearance, and clothing made only of khadi could be a sign of nationalism for men (although as we will see, very few men in the nationalist movement took up wearing only a loincloth).

Gandhi intended khadi to become a symbol of the "khadi spirit" that held national traits like patience, self-sacrifice, purity of faith, and a feeling of interconnection with other human beings. This was a nationalist vision because he was trying to dismantle gender and caste barriers that divided people. If everyone wore the same cloth and clothing styles, it would also be much more difficult for people to visually tell the caste and class of people when they first met. Indeed, Vijayalakshmi Pandit, Jawaharlal Nehru's sister, stated that she couldn't tell what class the visitors to her family's home belonged to—because they were dressed alike, and all of the Congressmen looked the same.[29] At the same time, Gandhi attempted to use khadi as a test of one's nationalist commitment. He claimed that anyone who wore foreign-made cloth was no longer Indian, and had essentially renounced their nationality.[30]

Some nationalists took up Gandhi's call and wore khadi in Indian-style clothing, such as Motilal Nehru, who had appeared in public in full and extravagant English dress before 1920. However, there was also pushback against khadi, even among nationalists. Some pointed out that even before mill-produced cloth had become the norm, Indian spinners and weavers had produced fine cloth made not only cotton but silk in a variety of colors. The coarse homespun khadi was therefore not necessarily traditional. Wealthier nationalists purchased very fine khadi, which was softer and less durable than coarser cloth, and others bought silk produced in India—swadeshi silk.

Perhaps the most visible dissent from khadi among nationalists was Sarojini Naidu. Naidu was already well-respected within the nationalist movement when Gandhi came back to India in 1915. She was a supporter of women's education and had participated in popularizing spinning among Indian women. However, she did not adopt khadi dress. A member of the elite, she preferred fine and expensive traditional materials, such as swadeshi silk. In making these choices, she was drawing upon a different vision of nationalism and swadeshi than Gandhi. She stated that buying luxury goods "means the giving of livelihood again to every craftsman—the dyer, the embroider, the goldsmith, the man who makes tassels for your weddings, the man who makes all the little things that you need for your home." In making this argument Naidu was reaching beyond cloth to all sorts of traditional craftsman, which was perhaps more practically encompassing of nationalist aims, although it

---

29. Susan S. Bean, "Gandhi and *Khadi*, Fabric of Independence," in *Cloth and the Human Experience*, ed. Weiner and Schneider, 355-376, 370–71; 373.

30. Tarlo, *Clothing Matters*, 89–90.

would not have served the same visually unifying purpose that Gandhi intended for khadi.[31] Interestingly, her argument was *not* based on gender stereotypes that held women to be delicate and thus in need of softer fabrics.

Gandhi's attempts to have a uniform clothing style for common people also did not really catch on. Many non-elite men from different religions continued to maintain different clothing, even if it was made from khadi. Hindus generally wore dhotis, kurtas, and Gandhi caps, while Muslims wore kurta pajamas with a cap or fez, and Sikhs still wore the turbans that were a sign of their faith. Parsi (who followed the Persian prophet Zoroaster) and Christian men generally did not wear khadi, and instead maintained European styles.[32]

For Hindu nationalist women, adopting khadi cloth and clothing was more complicated because white, homespun cloth—the two main characteristics of khadi—were symbols of widowhood, which was a degraded status. Most women who adopted khadi saris were from the middle and upper-class, who could add some type of decoration to it to avoid being mistaken for widows. We see this in the photo in Figure 4.2. Kasturba is dressed in a sari over a blouse. Because the photo is in black and white, it is difficult to tell what color the clothing is, but it is unlikely to have been pure white. And even if the cloth of Kasturba's sari was white, the motifs on it made it visually distinctive from a widow's sari. Over the course of the 1920s different groups also adopted khadi saris of the same color, including a group of female nationalists who wore black saris, with borders of green, orange, and red.[33]

In Egypt the Western suit served as a marker of modernity, and was particularly embraced by young *effendi*. Here, as in India, British colonial officials used dress to mark a distinction between themselves and Egyptians. This sparked a new consciousness in the press among authors and public commentators about the meanings of clothing. As was also the case in India, young Egyptians who dressed in Western manners were sometimes ridiculed. The author of an article in *al-Ajyal* from 1897 was critical of young Egyptians who thought that dressing like Westerners was the same as being modern and civilized. An article some months later added further critique—that such dress was usually expensive, and would lead to financial ruin for those who spent money on European clothing rather than more essential needs. The author also extended this to women, whom he chastised for putting pressure on their husbands and fathers to pay for women's Western clothing.[34]

Egypt was also heavily influenced by Turkey (both had been part of the Ottoman Empire), and the modernization reforms that Mustafa Kemal (Atatürk) enacted in the 1920s, particularly around clothing. In the early 1920s

31. Lisa Trivedi, *Clothing Gandhi's Nation: Homespun and Modern India* (Bloomington: Indiana University Press, 2007), 92.

32. Tarlo, *Clothing Matters*, 115.

33. Tarlo, *Clothing Matters*, 110–11.

34. Jacob, *Working Out Egypt*, 199–201.

Kemal implemented a series of dress reforms for Turkish people, including leg-islating that men wear Western-style suits, and strongly encouraging women to stop wearing veils. In 1925 Fikri Abaza, the editor of the Egyptian magazine *Al-Musawwar*, explained that the Turkish reforms in dress were interesting, but peripheral to whether a nation was truly modern. He saw Kemal's dress reforms for men as antidemocratic because they restricted personal choices. However, he did not extend this choice to women; Abaza focused on Kemal's wife, Latifa Hanim, who dressed in Western clothing, even arguing that it was Latifa's unveil-ing and participation in mixed company that caused their marriage to fail.[35]

Abaza's article provoked a response from the editor of the *Al-Nil al-Musawwar*, a newspaper that was pro-palace who called Abaza's statements extreme and shortsighted. The editor of the *al-Nil* defended Kemal's reforms, arguing that Western clothes were those required for a modern lifestyle as they were more effi-cient and allowed the wearer to be more productive. He also pointed out that the cost of a Western suit was less than half of a set of traditional *baladi* costume.[36]

The Top of the Body: Headwear

While Gandhi's efforts to get people to wear a uniform style of dress made of khadi may have had relatively limited success, his invention of the "Gandhi cap" became a symbol of Indian nationalism. As with clothing in general, British of-ficials used headwear to mark British civilization and the "other." There was no more iconic piece of British clothing accessory than the pith helmet, invented in the 1840s to protect Europeans from the tropical sun. Worn by women and children as well as men (although the former had fancier versions), the hat was so ubiquitous among Britons in India that Indians sometimes referred to them as "topi walas" or "hat-wearing people."[37]

Gandhi used khadi to make a style of hat that was traditionally from Kashmir (the region between what is today India and Pakistan). This was practical as well as symbolic. The cap covered the head, but it was cooler than other hats and was thin enough that it could be folded and placed in men's pockets because it was made from cotton instead of wool. Made from undyed cotton it was white, so it showed dirt easily and needed to be frequently washed, yet the material made it easily washable. Unlike the turbans that Indian men in many regions wore, the khadi cap also required much less cloth, and was therefore cheaper to make or buy.

By 1920, the khadi cap had caught on as a form of resistance to British authority. Gandhi delivered two different sets of messages about the cap, however: at times he

---

35. Jacob, *Working Out Egypt*, 203–04.

36. Jacob, *Working Out Egypt*, 205.

37. Tarlo, *Clothing Matters*, 32.

emphasized practicality and aesthetic simplicity, calling it a "beautiful, light, inoffensive" accessory, while at other times promoting it as a political symbol, stating that he hoped that "thousands will be prepared to die for the khadi cap which is fast becoming a visible mark of swadeshi and swaraj." By propagating both messages simultaneously, he was attempting to make the British government's repression of the cap look irrational and an overreaction to a simple fashion choice. British authorities were not persuaded that the cap was only a cap, and took the view of it as a political statement. In 1922, the chief justice at a high court in Ratnagiri banned the Gandhi cap and stated that those wearing it would be "guilty of disrespect to the Judge."[38]

The Gandhi cap may have also had interreligious origins as well as nationalist connections. Gandhi began wearing it during the Khalifat Movement (1919–1924) when Muslims in India protested the removal of the ruler of the Ottoman Empire after World War I, (the Sultan was considered by Sunni Muslims to be the spiritual leader of Islam as well as a political leader). Some historians assert that this was an attempt by Gandhi to reach out to Muslim Indians.[39] Indeed, the design of the Gandhi cap does resemble the fez, an important symbol of Ottoman and Muslim identity in the late 1800s and early 1900s.

The fez, however, also had its own nationalist trajectory. As part of Turkish modernization dress reforms after the removal of the Ottoman sultan, Kemal, gradually banned the fez in favor of Western-style hats over the course of the mid- late-1920s.[40] For Egyptians, however, the fez was a sign of Egyptian nationalism, as we can see in an incident in Turkey from 1932. On Turkish Republic Day, the Egyptian ambassador was invited to a celebration hosted by Kemal. The ambassador arrived dressed in his formal attire, wearing a fez. Because this was after the period when Kemal had banned the fez in Turkey, he ordered the Egyptian ambassador to remove it, which after some hesitation, he did. The ambassador's office attempted to keep the event quiet, but the incident was widely reported and caused public outrage in Egypt. Some demanded that Egypt to sever diplomatic relations with Turkey, and called the incident an affront to Egypt's national honor.[41]

As this incident shows, like the Gandhi cap, the fez could hold multiple meanings depending upon who was wearing one and what one thought of the wearer. The fez also reveals the tangled relationship between religion, politics, and "modernity" (which had imperial connotations). Islamic sumptuary laws (laws regulating clothing) stated that Muslims must dress in a way that would visually differentiate them from non-Muslims. What this clothing might look like, however, was flexible.

---

38. Tarlo, *Clothing Matters*, 84–85.

39. Bean, "Gandhi and *Khadi*," 367.

40. Patricia L. Baker, "The Fez in Turkey: A Symbol of Modernization?" *Costume: The Journal of the Costume Society* 20, no. 1 (1986): 72–85, 80.

41. Wilson Chacko Jacob, *Working Out Egypt: Effendi Masculinity and Subject Formation in Colonial Modernity, 1870–1940* (Durham, NC: Duke University Press, 2011), 186.

In 1827, Sultan Mahmud II (leader of the Ottoman Empire, which was broken into several countries including Egypt and Turkey after World War I) persuaded religious leaders to accept the wearing of the fez.[42] In 1829, Mahmud II's government issued a decree that only the *ulema*, or Islamic religious leaders, were exempt from wearing fez instead of turbans. This new ruling caused very little stir because by that time men in Istanbul, and the wealthy in other areas, had adopted many elements of European men's dress, discarding turbans for other types of headwear including the fez.

By the early twentieth century, for some Turkish nationalist leaders the fez had changed from a symbol of modernization for men to a symbol of Turkish backwardness, and thus Kemal banned it during his modernization and secularization of Turkey in the 1920s. In 1925, Kemal himself appeared in a tour of Anatolia first wearing a "Panama hat," a Western style brimmed hat, and then bare-headed while holding the hat. This broke religious norms of different clothing for Muslims and non-Muslims, and religious injunctions that men's heads should be covered unless they were performing certain religious rituals.

This was deeply disturbing to members of the ulema because they associated wearing a brimmed European hat with apostasy—meaning that a Muslim had converted to Christianity. In response to this, Kemal's government found a ruling from a *mufti* (an Islamic religious leader) in Cairo that stated that Muslim men were able to wear brimmed hats for climatic reasons and to conform to social pressure. However, Turks continued to resist the edict to wear Western-style hats, particularly the ulema. The government continued to arrest ulema members for disobedience well into the 1940s.[43]

The debate about whether the fez or Western hats were more suitable for men in Egypt was crystalized in a controversy in Cairo in 1926. In February of that year, students at the Islamic schools of Dar al-'Ulum (a prominent school for boys in Cairo) and Al-Azhar Maher (a prestigious university, also in Cairo) came to class wearing suits and fez. When the education minister attempted to enforce the dress code of robes and turbans, the students went on strike. Because these were Islamic schools, this was intimately tied to religious law. The minister secured *fatwa* (an opinion about religious law) from the *mufti* of Egypt and the rector of Al-Azhar that Western-style hats were un-Islamic. As had Kemal's Turkish government, the students also acquired *fatawa* from different scholars, stating that the only ruling in Islam about dress was to cover the naked body.[44] The Ministry of Education rejected the student's arguments and demanded that they return or face expulsion; the students eventually returned. However, the debate over clothing and what it meant in an Islamic culture rippled out into the larger society, as different newspapers and journals took up the question.

---

42. Baker, "The Fez in Turkey," 74.

43. Baker, "The Fez in Turkey," 80–82.

44. Jacob, *Working Out Egypt*, 206.

Here, as with clothing in general in an imperial context, the idea of "modernity" played a role, particularly in terms of the health of the body. One of the organizations that took up the question of the fez was the Eastern League (*al-Rabita al-Sharqiyya*), which asked the Egyptian Medical Association (EMA) to decide whether Western clothing or traditional clothing—particularly headwear—was more healthful for Egyptian men. The EMA caused controversy by ruling that in all cases, Western styles were better. In the case of headwear, like Kemal's reformers, the EMA stated that a pith helmet and brimmed hat, which would protect the skin from the sun, were healthier than the brimless fez.

The reaction to the EMA's statement was fierce. Ahmad Zaghlul, nephew of a nationalist hero Sa'd Zaghlul, condemned the EMA's ruling and pointed to the student strikes where Sa'd Zaghlul had told the students that "the question of dress is an issue of authentic national identity [*qawmiyya mahda*]. If we change our own [style] of dress, we would change our national identity, and a people without a national identity are a people without life."[45] In other words, to abandon the fez and don Western suits and hats was to abandon one's nationality. Ahmad Zaghlul also pointed that the EMA was not representative of Egyptian society and he dismissed their advice to only applying to a fraction of Egyptian men who had been Westernized. In contrast to these young men, Zaghlul argued that the EMA should be focused on the more pressing health concerns of the general peasantry—an effort that would "uplift your nation."[46]

Pan-Islamist activist Shakib Arsalan also condemned the EMA's ruling. He argued that if the EMA felt that Egyptians should emulate the West, then they should take on the entirety of Western lifestyle and not simply the clothing. Arsalan also argued that Egypt already had a variety of headwear and it would be too chaotic to add the Western hat. Instead, the inclusion of this visually non-Eastern hat would cause confusion and outsiders would see Egyptian society as "amorphous."[47]

For Egyptian women, the veil was as contentious as the fez and raised many of the same issues about modernity and gender. The opening salvo of this debate was launched by Qassim Amin in two books: *The Liberation of Women (Tahrir al-Mar'a)* in 1899 and *The New Woman (al-Mar'a al-jadida)* in 1900. In *The Liberation of Women*, Amin detailed reforms that he thought necessary in order for Egypt to advance as a nation, and that would benefit Muslim countries more generally. He focused on three reforms in particular: education for women, the veil, and the family (particularly polygamy). In the chapter on the veil, he explained that he was not advocating for its complete removal while noting that "the Shari'a does not stipulate the use of the veil." In fact, he asserted, "Islamic law has given the same rights to women as to men," including the right to

45. Jacob, *Working Out Egypt*, 208–09.

46. Jacob, *Working Out Egypt*, 210.

47. Jacob, *Working Out Egypt*, 211.

make contracts. Veiling hindered women's ability to have this right because it was too logistically difficult for people to discern a veiled woman's identity. Amin asked:

> How can a poor woman who is veiled take on a business or trade and earn a livelihood? How can a veiled maid render adequate service in a house in which there are men? How can a business woman administer her affairs in the midst of men? How can a veiled peasant woman cultivate her land or reap her crop? How can a veiled worker who has hired herself out as a builder possibly build a house or anything else?

Indeed, they could not; however, rather than not engaging in these activities because they were veiled, many peasant women simply did not wear veils. Sidestepping this practical reality, Amin based his argument on a "truer" interpretation of religious law, and asserted that Shari'a allowed for a woman's face and palms to be uncovered, as he stated that "I am not asking for more than what the Shari'a allows."[48]

Amin also presented veiling as a question of social progression of Egypt vis-à-vis the West: "Should we be satisfied with our present condition and accept the ways of our forefathers while others around us race toward happiness, the resources of comfort, and positions of strength, thus quickly overtaking us?" He argued that the veil was a "great hindrance to a woman's progress, and indeed to a country's progress." Amin claimed that the veil and seclusion at home at the onset of puberty stunted women's intellectual growth. Instead, women needed to not only learn from books, but also to encounter the world to assess the ideas contained within the books. In this Amin held up the example of Eastern Christian women who had not been sequestered, and "as a result their status has been raised higher than that of their Muslim compatriots, even though they are of the same sex and live in the same region."[49]

Amin also maintained that the veil and seclusion were not a guarantor of women's purity, pointing to the example of American women, and Bedouin and rural women in Egypt, who maintained morality despite regular contact with men. In contrast to this, Amin stated that it was "the secluded woman ... [who] is tempted by the mere sight of a man ... A glance is sufficient to kindle desire in her" because such contact was rare and forbidden.[50] Indeed, Amin argued that seclusion had achieved nothing, and there were often tales of immorality within Egyptian homes.

Instead, Amin argued that a "proper upbringing and an independent will are the two universally necessary factors for the progress of men. They are the desired goals of every nation in pursuit of happiness, and they are among the most noble means for attaining the perfection for which a nation is destined." Citing European history, Amin pointed to the use of the chastity belt during the Middle

---

48. Amin, *The Liberation of Women*, 37–41.

49. Amin, *The Liberation of Women*, 46–47; 49–50.

50. Amin, *The Liberation of Women*, 52.

Ages and stated that it was only when "women were released from their shackles to enjoy their new freedom and walk with their men, helping, supporting, and contributing their opinions on every facet of life," did Western civilization grow.[51]

He also compared the homes of Eastern and Westerners and found the Eastern homes (even middle-class) wanting, both aesthetically and economically, because seclusion essentially required building two houses, "one for men and one for women." Amin concluded by connecting nationalism to the liberation of women, stating that "a hatred of autocracy, a hostility toward subjugation, and a desire to direct human energy toward a specific goal are among the prevailing attitudes of our present era. It is therefore inevitable that women should receive their share of this generous spirit that moves among us reminding us of our forgotten rights."[52]

Scholars often see *The Liberation of Women* as the starting point for feminism in the Middle East. However, Amin's ideas were far from uncontested. By holding up the West as an example of how women *should* be treated, he was tapping into the rationale that Western men used to justify colonizing the East—the degraded position of women. British colonial officials and feminists, and male and female Christian missionaries argued that (as scholar Leila Ahmed stated), "all essentially insisted that Muslims had to give up their native religion, customs, and dress, or at least reform their religion and habits along the recommended lines, and for all of them the veil and customs regarding women were the prime matters requiring reform."[53] For these people, then, true reform within Islam was impossible.

Indeed, the majority of the responses to Amin were critical. Nationalists objected to his lauding of the West, his negative stereotypes of common Egyptian people and the ulama, and the proposal that women unveil. These objections weren't necessarily antifeminist, however, as demonstrated by a response to Amin in *Al-Liwa*, Mustapha Kamil's newspaper. The authors affirmed women's right to an education, and that women's education was necessary for the progress of the nation (not just for their families and sons, as Amin had argued). However, in terms of the veil, they asserted that Amin's proposal was merely an ill-considered attempt to imitate the West.[54]

Men, however, weren't the only ones who weighed in on Amin's proposals—women did too. By the early 1900s Egyptian women acquired formal education at increasing rates, formed women's organizations, and made their voices heard thanks to the boom in print culture. For example, Malak Hifni Nassef published articles in *Al-Jarida* (albeit under the pseudonym of Bahithat al-Badiyya, or Seeker in the Desert). Women were also active participants in political organizations and protests—some of them violent.

---

51. Amin, *The Liberation of Women*, 58.

52. Amin, *The Liberation of Women*, 56; 58–60.

53. Leila Ahmed, *Women and Gender in Islam: Historical Roots of a Modern Debate* (New Haven, CT: Yale University Press, 1992), 154.

54. Ahmed, *Women and Gender in Islam*, 163.

However, nationalist women had differing views when it came to topics such as the veil, and how best to accomplish nationalist and women's goals, as we see in the attitudes of Huda Sha'rawi and Malak Hifni Nassef towards veiling. In 1923 Sha'rawi and a group of women formed the Egyptian Feminist Union (EFU), which advocated for Egyptian self-rule and women's rights within the Egyptian constitution of 1923. Sha'rawi saw the veil as oppressive, and when she and her protégé returned from the International Women's Alliance meeting in Rome in 1923, they removed their veils as they stepped off the train in Cairo. As Ahmed argues, she was "politically nationalistic" in the sense that she believed in "gradual reform toward total political emancipation from British control and toward the adoption of Western political institutions and a secularist understanding of the state."[55]

In contrast to Sha'rawi, Malak Hifni Nassef opposed unveiling. While she did not believe that veiling was dictated by Shari'a, or that veiling was an indicator of a woman's modesty, she argued that women should not be pressured to unveil. She asserted that since veiling was the custom, women would have to get used to the idea, and men would have to change their behavior to not abuse women who were unveiled. In an echo of critiques that Amin was simply advocating for the imitation of Western norms, Nassef argued that the women who were currently unveiled were generally upper-class women who were not motivated by high-natured ideals such as liberty, but more concerned with fashion. Continuing in this vein, she argued that Western cultural norms warranted careful consideration before adoption, and that Egyptians should only embrace beneficial changes.

Conclusion

In this chapter, we have seen how nationalists used the body and clothing to attempt to create an identity that was distinctly national. We began by examining the politics of men's and women's bodies as political sites. For men, nationalism and masculinity were tied together perhaps most notably in the idea that men had to be physically fit and muscular. While this idea was present in many different areas in the late 1800s and early 1900s, in a colonial context it took on an extra layer of meaning as a rationale for who was "fit" to rule the nation. For Indian and Egyptian women, reforms based on sex and marriage—particularly child marriage, the age of consent, and polygamy—were the staging ground for discussions of nationalism and reform. Clothing and headwear also served as visible manifestations of nationalism, as khadi, Gandhi caps, and the fez illustrate. As these examples also show, these were not uncontested or simple meanings, nor were they universally accepted among nationalists themselves.

We learn several things by focusing on the physical body. Bodies are perhaps the most literal, and certainly the most visceral, aspect of the nation. Most nations have

---

55. Ahmed, *Women and Gender in Islam*, 171; 178.

the idea of birthright citizenship—that is, if one is born on the soil of a nation, one is a member of that nation. We also have the idea of citizenship being tied to residence within national boundaries, which allow for people to petition to become naturalized citizens. In the context of imperialism, however, these things are more tenuous in some ways. For example, can a person born from British-citizen parents in India be British, or are they Indian? This is revealed by the confusion of the term "Anglo-Indian," which generally means British people residing in India, and not a child of mixed British and Indian ancestry. The idea here is that British people retain their Britishness despite very long residences in India. However, because British colonial officials' ties to the physical land of Britain were unstable, other things came to stand in for colonizer's physical connections to the nation, such as home (as we saw in chapter 3 with the French Empire) and here, clothing.

For nationalists, the body and the clothing that covered it could also be used to create ties between people. Nationalists did this in one of two ways. One way was to evoke a past tradition or symbol, such as Swami Vivekananda's Hindu warrior monk ethos, or Gandhi's return to preindustrial khadi cloth. Another way nationalists created identity was to create something new and to argue that this way was fresh, modern, and free of the cultural baggage that might divide groups within the nation. Gandhi and the Tagores did this with their proposals of new styles of clothing, and Indian nationalist women did this more successfully with new women's organizations such as the All-India Women's Conference.

Finally, the body and clothing as symbols of the nation demonstrate that the methods for building nationalism that other scholars have identified, such as print capitalism and state-run schools, may not have been necessary. In a large population where illiteracy rates were high, and where there were no state-run schools or similar institutions to build common ground between people, nationalists had other avenues to build solidarity—such as customs around the body and clothing.

FURTHER READING

Bannerjee, Sukanya. *Becoming Imperial Citizens: Indians in the Late-Victorian Empire.* Durham, NC: Duke University Press, 2010.

Baron, Beth. *Egypt as a Woman: Nationalism, Gender and Politics.* Berkeley: University of California Press, 2007.

Keddie, Nikki R. *Women in the Middle East: Past and Present.* Princeton, NJ: Princeton University Press, 2007.

Pollard, Lisa. "The Family Politics of Colonizing and Liberating Egypt, 1882–1919." *Social Politics* 7, no. 1 (Spring 2000): 47–79.

Sarkar, Sumit, and Tanika Sarkar. *Women and Social Reform in Modern India: A Reader.* Bloomington: Indiana University Press, 2008.

Sinha, Mrinalini. *Specters of Mother India: The Global Restructuring of an Empire.* Durham, NC: Duke University Press, 2006.

GENDER, SOFT POWER, AND THE WESTERN IN COLD WAR EUROPE

In the fall and early winter of 2004, I was conducting dissertation research in Geneva, Switzerland, and happened to be there on December 11 for the festival of L'Escalade. The event celebrates the moment in 1602 when the residents of Geneva repelled an attack by the duke of Savoy. As part of the celebration children dress up in costumes, as they would for the Halloween in the United States, and walk around collecting coins for charities. I took advantage of a day off from research in the archives to go up in the tower of the St. Pierre Cathedral, which has a commanding view of the city. As I looked down upon the nearby square, my eye was caught by a boy in a stereotypical Native American feathered headdress, running around and appearing to be having a great time.

I confess that I was surprised by the sight of that boy in an outfit that signified something so prototypically American—the US West. I shouldn't have been. Europe has a long history of embracing myths about the American frontier. From Buffalo Bill's Wild West Show, which toured Europe and the Middle East in the late 1800s and early 1900s, to the film *True Grit*, which was nominated for Best Film in the British Academy of Film and Television Arts awards in 2010, the US West has long been incorporated into European popular culture. In addition to US cultural productions of the West, Europeans have also embraced the genre, such as Germany's Karl May, who wrote fictionalized accounts of interactions between Apache and Western settlers.

While Westerns had been a staple of filmmaking since the turn of the century, they peaked in popularity during the Cold War (1945–1989)— an ideological struggle between the Soviet Union (USSR) and United States (US) about who would be the primary global economic, cultural, and social influence. The Cold War also ushered in the emergence of a new world order—in the wake of World War II, nationalist movements such as those in India were successful, and many colonies gained independence (seventeen African colonies became independent nations in 1960). The US and USSR competed for influence over those countries (known as "unaligned" nations) who were not directly allied with either superpower. Sometimes these American and Soviet attempts to attract allies were coercive and led to bitter divisions and armed conflict among the populations of these new states.

As global support for formal imperialism faded, anticolonial nationalist movements gained momentum across the globe, and decolonization in Asia and Africa increased in political force within global institutions like the United Nations and in public opinion, it became clear that formal colonization was untenable. As the Vietnam War, and the massive demonstrations against it in the US showed, putting "boots on the ground" was not only unpopular but also financially and politically damaging to the US.

As part of the Cold War, US officials therefore attempted to spread influence around the world through "soft power"—cultural outreach and financial aid packages. The US State Department sponsored tours of jazz musicians and sports stars, as well as individual-level diplomatic programs such as People to People and the Peace Corps. Products from US corporations flooded postwar Europe as part of the massive infusion of capital popularly called the Marshall Plan, and spread to other areas of the world as part of US aid and development packages. And US film and television productions were viewed by millions of people.

While many of these films and television programs were set in their present day, a significant number also rehashed the past, or used it loosely as a setting for plots. One of the most consistent of these were Westerns. The plot lines of Westerns were generally simplistic. Westerns portrayed the US Western frontier as a desolate, barren place where hardy men and sometimes women fought against a harsh environment, outlaws, and marauding Indians in order to create a life for themselves. Writers and directors used the seeds of real historical experiences to create a fictional world where they could set archetypal characters, including the warrior, the mentor, and others. In this way, the "West" became both abstract (similar to the way that we view outer space; it's no coincidence that the *Star Wars* trilogy has sometimes been described as a "space Western") even as it also became almost a synonym for the US, as though all of the country were this fictionalized West.

Make no mistake about it, though: Westerns were a celebration of the imperialism of Manifest Destiny. They promoted the idea that US expansion across continental North America was one of divine right, rather than of violent settler colonialism in which indigenous peoples were forcibly removed from land so that Euro-Americans could occupy it. This idea of the divinity of European settlement is clear in John Gast's painting *American Progress* (1872), which portrayed a celestial being (in this case a Greco-Roman type goddess) leading ranchers, farmers, and settlers in a covered wagon West. Fleeing before her (and them) into darkness were Native Americans and wild animals. Following behind were the hallmarks of modern civilization—railroads, telegraph lines, and cities.

This idea of the West as synonymous with US identity was further enshrined at the 1893 Chicago World's Fair, when the historian Frederick Jackson Turner gave a speech titled "The Significance of the Frontier in American History." Turner theorized that westward progression of Euro-Americans took place in a series of stages inexorably moving west: fur trappers and traders encountered Native Americans and the wilderness, paving the way for ranchers, who then gave way to farmers, who in turn were replaced by cities and industrial manufacturing. Turner believed that this process—the encounter with the "frontier"—was what gave Americans their distinctive character. Faced with the harsh physical conditions of the West (the environment, the isolation from other Europeans, threats from Native Americans and wild animals), European settlers were forced to undergo a Darwinian process—either evolve and adapt to the new conditions by becoming American, or die.

These ideas of the West and the frontier in the late 1800s were from a decidedly Euro-centric viewpoint, and portrayed indigenous peoples as obstacles to be faced and overcome in the process of European settlement. By the Cold War, the general popular culture vision of the West and the frontier was more complex. For one thing, very few Euro-Americans would have been willing to "play Indian" during the mid-1800s. However, by the Cold War, many Euro-Americans had practiced playing Indian, dressing up in what they interpreted as indigenous costumes, mimicking the dances and songs of some tribes, and spending time in teepees in the woods. These activities became popular in the early 1900s, as scouting movements in the US stressed the need for Euro-American children to come into regular contact with the outdoors to offset the potential ill effects of city life and overcivilization (a redux of the arguments about neurasthenia from chapter 3).

Indeed, many hobbyists who played Indian also did so *because* of the Cold War. In addition to concerns about technology and where it was leading the world (particularly in the case of atomic weapons and power), many Euro-Americans felt alienated by post–World War II life. For white, middle-class men, the period of the Cold War was fraught with highly charged choices. Popular culture and government advice pressured them to be economic providers, even while they often felt like cogs in a machine or invisible completely, as portrayed in the play *Death of a Salesman* by Arthur Miller. Images of fatherhood pervaded television (*Leave it to Beaver* was just one example of many), and yet men couldn't be *too* nurturing or sympathetic or they risked becoming "soft" and therefore potentially communist, at least according to Senator Joseph McCarthy, who decried "egg sucking phony liberals."[1] In this balancing act of masculinity, Western films and television shows offered a simplistic and homosocial (people interacting with members of only one sex) way for men to "escape" from their regular lives. Westerns of all types were popular—over 10 percent of published works were Westerns, and eight of the top television shows were Westerns, such as *The Lone Ranger* (1947–1957) and *Bonanza* (1959–1973).[2]

While some searched for themselves in the roles of the "cowboy," playing Indian was also part of some men's search for authenticity, in which middle-class Euro-Americans did things like travel, take drugs, make art, and drop out of "mainstream"

---

1. Michael Kimmel, *Manhood in America: A Cultural History* (London: The Free Press, 1996), 236.

2. Kimmel, *Manhood in America*, 252.

US society. These were the hippies of the 1960s and early 1970s, who hoped to essentially find themselves while in the process of playing racial "others." This authenticity was almost always inward looking, however, and not about coming into contact with real, live Native Americans—who by 1968 were advocating for their own rights in the American Indian Movement (AIM)—but instead having all of the stereotypical *stuff* that US popular culture associated with Indians such as the clothing and headdresses, the beads, the shells, the teepees, and the war clubs.[3] In other words, instead of addressing the legacies of the actual historic process of imperialism that violently removed Native people from their territory, the fictionalized versions of the West and Native Americans allowed Euro-Americans to project their own concerns and tropes into a sanitized, imaginary, and timeless space.

Given the tremendous impact of decolonization and the liberation of peoples, whom Europeans and Americans would have described as "backward" and "barbaric" not so long before the Cold War, it is ironic that one of the most-exported film genres around the world during the Cold War should be Westerns. We might see this as a fundamental mistake on the part of the US government, who supported the export of films and Hollywood filmmakers. And yet Westerns seem to have been both popular and influential around the world perhaps because the frontier *could* be detached from its geographic location and distilled into more simple narrative modes, such as the quest narrative. For example, the Mauritanian filmmaker Abderrahmane Sissako, whose work has won prizes at the French Cannes Film festival and been nominated at the US Academy Awards, was influenced by the so-called Italian spaghetti Westerns that were shown in theaters when he was a teenager.[4] The various types of Westerns reveal the flexibility of the genre, and the subtle ways that Westerns differed by country of origin— "spaghetti" Westerns (Italian), "charro" Westerns (Mexican), and the "ramen" Western (from Asia). There are also Westerns made in Australia and India.

As we will see in the course of this chapter, their very malleability made Westerns a type of blank slate onto which filmmakers and government officials could impart political messages. Here we will be focusing on Westerns made in the US and in East and West Germany to examine the ways that these films show gender ideals (particularly masculinity) and the intersection of those ideals with race and imperialism. I have selected East and West Germany because they had a shared past before the Cold War, spoke the same language, and to a certain extent shared cultural programming (at least as far as West German radio and television waves could reach into East Germany). However, as we see from Map 5.1, they were divided by the Cold War. West

---

3. See Philip Deloria, *Playing Indian* (New Haven, CT: Yale University Press, 1998).

4. Tsitsi Jaji, "Cassava Westerns: Ways of Watching Abderrahmane Sissako," *Black Camera* 6, no. 1 (Fall 2014), 154–177.

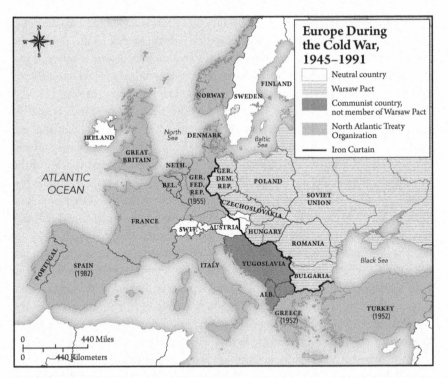

MAP 5.1 Europe During the Cold War, 1945–1991

Germany was capitalist, and East Germany was under the control of the USSR and was communist. The differences in their political ideologies shaped the messages about gender norms, which they projected through their films set in the US West.

The Archetypal Cowboy

There are three films that we will examine that show different types of masculinity— John Wayne's roles in *Red River* (1948) and *The Searchers* (1956), and the various roles in *The Magnificent Seven* (1960). I have selected two John Wayne films because he was immensely popular and well-known in Europe. In 1950 he was awarded the French Grand Prix-Film de Français Award for the most popular foreign star, and in 1953 a Hollywood Foreign Press Association poll named him the most popular actor in the world. German director Wim Wenders asserted that Wayne was "the most popular American actor ever to appear on the screen in Germany."[5]

_____

5. Russell Meeuf, *John Wayne's World: Transnational Masculinity in the Fifties* (Austin: University of Texas Press, 2013) 4–5.

Wayne portrayed the type of masculinity that became associated with the political character of US: physically tough, assertive, convinced that he was right in the face of opposition from others, individualistic, and leader of groups that were dominated by men, some of whom also had strong personalities (a leader among leaders). In *Red River* Wayne played Thomas Dunson, an aspiring cattle rancher who joins a wagon train headed for California.[6] At the Texas border, Dunson and his friend Groot (Walter Brennan) leave the train, which is then attacked by Indians. In the morning a boy named Matthew Garth (Montgomery Clift) emerges from the sagebrush, having escaped the massacre. Dunson takes on responsibility of the boy, although he makes it clear that they are not a family. After traveling for several more days, and upon deciding that he has found the perfect land that he wants, Dunson violently fights off men from "the Don" who owns the land, and claims it (essentially a shortened repetition of the Mexican-American War).

The film then moves forward fifteen years; Dunson has a significant number of cattle, but is facing financial ruin with the collapse of the cattle market after the Civil War. He decides to attempt to drive his ten thousand cattle to Missouri, where he can sell them for a higher price. He gathers a troop of cowboys, but in the long and difficult trip Dunson becomes a brutal tyrant. Eventually the cowboys, led by Garth, mutiny against him and change the destination to Abilene, Kansas, where they have word of a new railroad terminal. The men abandon Dunston, who vows to give chase and to kill Garth. On their way to Abilene, Garth and the cowboys encounter a wagon train headed for Nevada that is being attacked by Indians. They come to the defense of the whites, and in the process Garth meets his love interest (and practically the only woman) of the film, Tess (Joanne Dru). After saving the wagon train, Garth and the other cowboys reach Abilene, where there is indeed a rail terminal and where a cattle-broker from Illinois is anxious to give them a high price for all of their cows (making Garth a better businessman than Dunson).

Meanwhile, Dunson catches up to the Nevada wagon train and agrees to take Tess to Abilene. Once there, Dunson confronts Garth, and shoots at him without hitting him, as Garth refuses to fire back. They then have a fistfight, which is broken up by Tess, who says that she had been afraid for Garth's life but she should have realized that the two loved each other and wouldn't kill each other. At this point Dunson admits a respect for Garth, and says he will add Garth's initials to the ranch's brand.

In comparison to the versions of masculinity that would come in later Westerns, Dunson is a surprisingly harsh character, perhaps because he has multiple foes and obstacles rather than a single one or group. In dealing with subordinates, whether close associates such as Groot (who is subordinate despite having

---

6. As I discuss the events in the films, I will use the present tense (following the conventions of other disciplines for whom the work is in a state of eternal present), as well as when I discuss parts of the film.

been with Dunson for the entire film and being older) Garth, or the subordinate cowboys in his employ, Dunson maintains violent authority. When his word or orders are questioned, his first instinct is to shoot or kill the man. On the trail, both Groot and Garth both tell him that he is being too extreme, but he doesn't change his behavior. In fact, he mocks Garth, saying that his "heart is too soft."

This type of masculinity also rejects ties to anyone else. Dunson's love interest dies in the first moments of the film, and there is no indication that he has any other romantic interests. In fact, he is blatantly misogynistic—when he meets Tess, he has her stand up and turn in a full circle so that he can look at her body. He then declares that since he no longer has a son (having disavowed Garth), he will give her half of the ranch if she can provide him with one.

Even among the other men, Dunson didn't have any friends. Groot deserts him to go with Garth to Abilene, and when Dunson arrives in Abilene he comes with hired guns who are simply there to provide fire power. At the end of the film, beyond the fact that Dunson is planning to add Garth's initials to the brand (essentially reinstating him as a son), there is no indication that Dunson is going to change his behavior. There is no speech saying that he has learned that other people have value, that Garth was right to head to Abilene, or that he will listen to Garth in the future. There are no physical actions that indicate that he has softened—no hugs or handshakes with Garth or Groot, or anyone else.

Wayne's character in *Red River* embodies a central tension of the Cold War that we have examined earlier—the tension between an alliance with a woman that meant family and fatherhood, and the homosocial world of men working alongside each other.[7] Dunson shows this ambivalence when he attempts to create a family with Garth even though he is deeply conflicted about it. Instead, it is the younger, "softer" Garth who is potentially able to be both in a relationship with a woman and maintain homosocial work environments.

Coming shortly after the end of World War II in 1945, *Red River* was also a manifestation of how the US wanted to portray itself to the world—as heroic and destined to take up the mantle of civilization within an imperial context. In the intervening three years since the end of World War II, tensions between the US and USSR had ratcheted up dramatically and US officials had begun to crystalize the character of the USSR as being in opposition to the American way of life. For example, in 1946 diplomat George Kennan wrote his "Long Telegram," followed by an article in 1947 titled "The Sources of Soviet Conduct," in *Foreign Affairs* magazine, in which he argued that the USSR was fundamentally irrational and conflict-oriented toward capitalism, only understood the language of force, and was inherently expansionist. In this framework, the solitary and (unreasonably) persistent masculinity portrayed by the characters of Dunson and Garth in *Red River* reflected the larger status of the US within the world: standing strong

---

7. Meeuf, *John Wayne's World*, 18.

without many allies (Europe was still decimated by war) against a multifaced and fluid enemy.

Even though it came twelve years after *Red River*, Wayne's character in *The Searchers*, Ethan Edwards, projected a similar type of masculinity as Dunson's. In the film, Edwards arrives home to his brother's ranch in Texas five years after the Civil War. Although he doesn't say where he has been, the implication is that he has been fighting Native Americans in the "Indian Wars" in the US West. Edwards is greeted by his brother, his brother's wife, their three children—two girls and a boy—and their adopted son Martin Pawley (Jeffrey Hunter), whom Edwards found in the sagebrush after his parents were killed by Native Americans. Like the character of Dunson in *Red River*, Edwards disavows kinship with Pawley, greeting him with the comment "don't call me uncle. I ain't your uncle" and reiterating throughout the film that Pawley is *not* part of the Edwards family.

Soon after Edwards's arrival, he, Pawley, and men from the neighboring ranches are lured away from the area, and the Edwards homestead is attacked by Comanche in a murder-raid. Edwards's brother, his brother's wife, and their son are killed at the ranch, and their two daughters are kidnapped. Edwards, Pawley, and the neighbors set out to get the girls back, and the film covers their years-long search.

Much like Dunston in *Red River*, Edwards rejects anyone else's authority over him. One of the neighbors is Edwards's former commander in the Civil War, and a figure of authority within the community as a reverend and a leader of the local group of Texas Rangers. Edwards struggles with him for control over the searchers, eventually fracturing the group, with the neighbors returning back to their homesteads. This leaves Edwards in clear command over the younger men Pawley, and Brad (the suitor of the eldest daughter); continuing on the search, Edwards tells them, "I'm giving the orders, and you're following them."

After many years of searching (during which Brad is killed by Native Americans), Edwards and Pawley do eventually find Debbie (Natalie Wood), the youngest daughter, and they take her "home" to the Jorgenson ranch. In the end however, it is unclear whether Edwards will be part of the continuing story. As Pawley, Debbie, and the Jorgensons go to the house, Edwards remains outside. The final scene in the film is Edwards walking away, framed by the open doorway as the theme song "Ride Away" plays. The song is also sung at the beginning of the film and includes the lyrics "What makes a man to wander? What makes a man to roam? What makes a man leave bed and board and turn his back on home? Ride away, ride away, ride away." In other words, while some of the male characters—Jorgensen, Pawley, and other neighbors—may be built for family life and home, the implication is that Edwards is not.

Like *Red River*, *The Searchers* reflected its time. By the mid-1950s the US had faced some stunning losses in the Cold War, with the communist revolution in China (1949), the stalemate of the Korean War (1950–1953), and the fall of much of Eastern Europe to Soviet influence. The US had redirected foreign policy from that of overcoming the USSR to containing the expansion of communism (symbolized in the report by the National Security Council known as NSC 68). The USSR had atomic weapons by 1949, making it equal to the arms capabilities of the US, and the US was embroiled in the "Red Scare" as Wisconsin congressman Joseph McCarthy attempted to root out alleged communist sympathizers throughout American society, including in the US military and government.

The Searchers shows these concerns. Rather than overcoming Native Americans, the Euro-American settlers in *The Searchers* seek to simply coexist with them. Paralleling the US characterization of the USSR are the Comanche, who provoke the fight that the settlers would rather avoid. Like international organizations such as the United Nations, the official community leader character in *The Searchers*—the reverend and former Texas Rangers officer—is weak in the face of aggression, and it is up to Edwards to continue with the task at hand. Finally, in the wake of the Korean War, which was essentially fought to a stalemate, the violence in *The Searchers* seems somewhat arbitrary and does not justify the ends.[8]

As both *Red River* and *The Searchers* show, the main type of masculinity was that of John Wayne's characters—individualistic, unemotional, prone to violence when angered, and dismissive of any man who didn't exhibit these qualities. However, there *were* other men in both of the films who did not display that type of masculinity and instead were less violent, opting for connections with their peers and showing compassion instead of impatience toward others. The characters of Garth and Pawley demonstrate this other masculinity—which could potentially be seen as the masculinity of the future West, which was more settled than the frontier.

In contrast to the types of complex masculinity (violent yet protective, for instance) on display in Wayne's roles, by the 1960s US filmmakers were beginning to simplify characters and plots. *The Magnificent Seven* (1960) therefore revolves around three groups of men: the farmers in a small, poor town south of the Mexican–US border; the bandits who are exacting tribute from them; and the group of US gunmen whom the farmers hire to kill the bandits. Although there is some complexity, the groups are fairly archetypal. The farmers are peaceable, family-oriented, and primarily concerned about the crops and livestock, protecting their farms and families. The gunmen are (with one exception) tough, prone to violence, and good at shooting to kill when provoked. The bandits are parasites, producing nothing of their own—neither food nor families—but instead

---

8. Stanley Corkin, *Cowboys as Cold Warriors: The Western and U.S. History* (Philadelphia: Temple University Press, 2004). See especially chapter 1, "Cowboys, Free Markets, Wyatt Earp and Thomas Dunson: *My Darling Clementine* and *Red River*," and chapter 4, "Korea, Containment, and Nationalism: *High Noon*, *Shane*, and *The Searchers*."

living off others and using the threat of wanton death and destruction of the farmers' families to get it. Film posters, such as the one in Figure 5.1, generally focused on the "magnificent seven" gunmen as a single masculine unit (although Yul Brynner is highlighted at the center):

FIGURE 5.1 *Magnificent Seven* movie poster (1960).
Source: SilverScreen / Alamy Stock Photo

One of the interesting aspects of the story arc of *The Magnificent Seven* is who ends up being depicted as winning. As the villains, the bandits are (of course) destroyed, but so are the majority of the seven gunslingers. The movie portrays them as a part of the fading West: men whose day has come and gone. The reason they go to the Mexican town, despite the very low wages that the farmers can pay, is that they cannot get work gunfighting elsewhere and they are not particularly inclined to take up more peaceful occupations. In the process of fighting the bandits, almost all of the seven are killed—the only ones left riding off into the sunset are Chris Adams (played by Yul Brynner) and Vin Tanner (Steve McQueen). While Chico (Horst Buchholz) survives, he chooses to go back to his farmer roots by staying in the village with his love interest, who is the only prominent female character in the film. As the old man who lives near the town remarks, the farmers—representing the settled, nonviolent, community-oriented masculinity—always win.

By posing one group of men as belonging to a violent past and the other group as belonging to the peaceful, progressive future, *The Magnificent Seven* shows the context of the Cold War in the late 1950s and early 1960s. During this time, the US switched away from direct conflicts with the USSR and instead focused on attracting developing nations to capitalism and US influence. This was expressed in funding development and modernization programs, and aid to unaligned nations, such as with the Peace Corps, agricultural technology, and population control advice. As in *The Magnificent Seven* when the gunmen yield to the farmers, US leaders portrayed the nation as dispensing justice and righting wrongs in other countries, but stepping back and allowing the local people (with appropriate training) to take up their own affairs again.

Westerns in West and East Germany

By the time of the Cold War the myth of the US West had been alive for decades in Europe. In the case of Germany, novelists such as Karl May (1842–1912) and journalists and amateur ethnographers such as Rudolf Cronau (1855–1939) spread the idea of the US West in the late 1800s and early 1900s. They were themselves working in the tradition of American fiction writers, such as the novelist James Fenimore Cooper in the early 1800s and poets like Henry Wadsworth Longfellow, from the mid-1800s.

Karl May's most famous books were a series of novels set in the American West that he alleged to be true, although he didn't visit there until later in his life. The books were incredibly popular—selling more than 100 million copies worldwide—and were translated into over thirty languages.[9] May's Western novels centered around the character of Old Shatterhand, a German living in

---

9. Pawel Goral, *Cold War Rivalry & The Perception of the American West* (London: Palgrave Macmillan, 2014), 2.

the West, and his Apache chief "blood brother" Winnetou. May portrayed Old Shatterhand and his fellow Germans (who were then settling on dispossessed Native American land) as fundamentally good, and instead placed the blame for violence and conflict on lawless whites. Native Americans in May's novels generally appear as the doomed and generally peaceful "noble savage" as compared the violent, exploitative rapist Comanche in *The Searchers*. However, like the portrayals of the West in *Red River* and *The Searchers*, May's frontier is almost entirely male, with female characters in peripheral roles.

May's Winnetou books, and his works more generally, reflect their historical context. As we saw in chapter 3, the late 1800s were the high point of European imperial expansion backed by Orientalist stereotypes that portrayed people in North Africa, the Middle East, and Asia as fundamentally backward. In both May's series of *Orient Cycle (Orientzyklus)* books (set in the Middle East and revolving around a murder mystery) and the Winnetou books, May consistently attempted to model how he thought colonizers should behave: not by employing brute force, but instead using knowledge, compassion, and psychology.[10] These ideas were in line with social Darwinist thinking about racial superiority. In this, there were certain races that could not adapt to modern life and would therefore inevitably face extinction. It was therefore the "white man's burden" (in Rudyard Kipling's phrase) to "lift up" these nonwhite races and "help" them become modern (e.g., capitalist, monogamous, agriculturally or factory oriented), or to witness their unavoidable extinction.

Despite claims to authenticity, May's accounts were largely fiction. Had he visited the US earlier he might have had the same experience as Rudolf Cronau, who became disillusioned when he toured America and wrote of his experience in the German publication *The Gazebo* (*Die Gartenlaube*) in 1881. While visiting a Sioux settlement outside of Fort Snelling, Minnesota, Cronau was enchanted by the "wigwams" but quickly disappointed that the world US novelist James Fennimore Cooper (who had been writing in the early 1800s) described had essentially disappeared. Native Americans Cronau saw did not wear moccasins; they wore European-style clothing and shoes. In the Dakotas he met not the young, lithe women of Longfellow's *The Song of Hiawatha* but instead Pa-Chu-Ta, the daughter of the Sioux woman Aya-ya-man-ka-wan, whom he described as "an enormous mass of flesh."[11] In contrast to his disappointment with Sioux women, Cronau was enchanted with male Sioux dancers, whom he saw outside of Fort Yates. Here were the Indians with painted faces, carrying weapons

10. Nina Berman, "Orientalism, Imperialism, and Nationalism: Karl May's Orientzyklus," in *The Imperialist Imagination: German Colonialism and Its Legacy*, ed. Sara Friedrichsmeyer, Sara Lennox, and Susanne Zantop (Ann Arbor: University of Michigan Press, 1998), 51–68, 59–60.

11. H. Glenn Penny, *Kindred by Choice: Germans and American Indians since 1800* (Chapel Hill: University of North Carolina Press, 2013), 103.

that Cronau expected. He wrote that "here, as I saw the dancers naked, I had the opportunity to marvel at the veritable athletic and superbly-built bodies of the Indians."[12] By the 1910s, however, Cronau had taken on a more paternalistic view of Native Americans: they need not be destroyed as the buffalo had, but instead could be transformed into useful workers.

While May was incredibly popular in the late 1800s and early 1900s, by the time of the Cold War his place in German culture had become more contentious because of World War II, and the fact that he had been a favorite author of Adolf Hitler. In fact Hitler, Joseph Goebbels (Reich Minister of Propaganda in Nazi Germany), and Hermann Göring (head of the Nazi air force, and later head of the military or *Reichsmarschall*) were all fans of May's novels. Hitler not only encouraged schools to use May's early books (not the later pacifist ones) to teach ideas such as military fitness and racial theory, but also that his military officers study Old Shatterhand's tactics.[13] According to Hitler's close associates, he reread May's novels periodically, remembered bits of trivia from them (with which he would regale visitors), and in one instance overruled his military general's objections to a decision with "they should have read Karl May."[14]

In the wake of World War II East and West Germany each dealt with their shared Nazi past differently, as we can see through their adaptations of May's works and Westerns in general. While Hitler may have overtly praised the military tactics in the Winnetou series, there was also no escaping that the same threads of social Darwinism ran through both the "natural" decline of the Native Americans in May's novels and the eugenics (the idea that state officials can "breed better people") and genocide of the Holocaust. The difference here was in whether or not "inferior" groups of people would be "allowed" to decline "naturally," or whether they would be forcibly removed from society and killed.

West German filmmakers attempted to mitigate the associations between May and the Nazis by hiring an American, Lex Barker, to play Old Shatterhand. Barker had in fact fought in World War II, been captured by the Nazis, and escaped from a POW camp. He was tall and blonde (a fact that didn't escape the German press) and athletic, and before the Winnetou films he had played in the role of another colonizing hero: Tarzan.[15] Winnetou was played by the French actor Pierre Brice. The directors also made subtle changes to the action within the films to make the characters seem less aggressive. As Pawel Goral explains in his

---

12. Quoted in Penny, *Kindred by Choice*, 107.

13. Franz A. Birgel, "The Only Good Indian is a DEFA Indian: East German Variations on the Most American of All Genres," in *International Westerns: Re-Locating the Frontier*, ed. Cynthia J. Miller and A. Bowdoin Van Riper (Lanham: Scarecrow Press, 2014), 37–62, 46.

14. Goral, *Cold War Rivalry*, 20–21.

15. Goral, *Cold War Rivalry*, 26–27.

book *Cold War Rivalry and the Perception of the American West*, "vigorous physicality of characters was reduced to a minimum, whereas aggression and power either belonged to the young generation or had a negative connotation and was associated with the antagonists."[16]

Goral also argues that the Winnetou films helped West Germans deal with their Nazi past and the Holocaust. In the main story arc of the series, Old Shatterhand and Winnetou become blood brothers, and Old Shatterhand sides with the Apache against desperadoes. Since the hero in the films sided with the underdog/victims, the Winnetou films helped mitigate Germans' sense of shame from the Holocaust. Instead, the audience was able to use the fictive events in the films to side with the heroes. This also fit in well with the West German government's official stance that ordinary Germans had resisted the Nazis. That being said, those who were familiar with the May novels tended to draw firmer connections between the racial decline of Native Americans in the novels and the Holocaust, and were therefore more critical of the Winnetou films.[17]

The eleven Winnetou films produced in West Germany were released over a period of four years, from 1962 to 1965, beginning with *Treasure of Silver Lake (Der Schatz im Silbersee)*. In this film, Old Shatterhand and Winnetou hunt for lost treasure. The film opens with the murder of Mr. Engel, who holds part of a treasure map, by bandits. Mr. Engel's son, Fred (Götz George), vows revenge when he hears of the murder and gets into a fight with Old Shatterhand. Winnetou, Old Shatterhand, Fred, and a motley group of others (a German colonial and a famous German "prairie poet") set off to beat the bandits to Butler's farm, where the other half of the map is being kept. Old Shatterhand's group arrives at the farm just before the bandits, who then surround the Butler's homestead (which has a reinforced stockade) and take Mr. Patterson hostage, as well as his daughter Ellen (Karin Dor), who happens to be outside of the homestead when the bandits arrive. Old Shatterhand and Fred make a daring rescue of Ellen and her father, but the bandits respond by mounting a full-scale attack on the homestead. Just when the bandits appear to be winning, a group of Osage warriors arrives to save the occupants and are greeted by Winnetau, who proclaims that "the Osages are our friends." Mrs. Butler (Marianne Hoppe), the widow owner of the farm, thanks the Osage chief, who then leaves with his warriors.

With the bandits in disarray, Old Shatterhand's group sets off for the valley where the treasure is located. On the way, however, they happen upon an Indian village that has been destroyed. As they are examining the wreckage, the warriors return and attack Old Shatterhand's group, assuming that they were the ones who murdered the Indian women and children. Ellen's horse bolts, and she is captured by the bandits. Old Shatterhand's group attempt to shoot the horses rather

16. Goral, *Cold War Rivalry*, 27.

17. Goral, *Cold War Rivalry*, 30.

than the warriors, forcing the enemy warriors to retreat as Old Shatterhand yells, "we're friends! Friends of the Indian."

Meanwhile, the bandits have taken Ellen to their base camp and have put her in a church for safety (although there is also the implication of sexual violence, as several bandits leer at her through a window). Old Shatterhand's group devises a plot whereby Fred—who has the treasure map memorized—will go to the bandit's camp and protect Ellen, and very slowly lead the bandits toward the treasure. In the meantime, Old Shatterhand's group will make their way to the valley and prepare an ambush.

However, things do not go as planned. The Utah, whose village was burned, capture Old Shatterhand and the chief, Big Wolf (Jozo Kovacevic), demands that Old Shatterhand be judged by the tribal council for killing the people in the village. Everyone in Old Shatterhand's group is taken to the Utah village, where Old Shatterhand manages to negotiate a type of trial by combat against Big Wolf. Old Shatterhand defeats Big Wolf, but instead of killing him knocks him unconscious, declaring that he is a "friend of the red men." Old Shatterhand's group then leaves the camp, but are pursued by a band of thirty Utah warriors who did not accept Old Shatterhand's victory, led by a troublemaker named Rolling Thunder (Slobodan Dimitrijevic).

Although only Rolling Thunder has a gun, Old Shatterhand's group has little hope of defeating so many warriors, and Old Shatterhand and Winnetou devise a plan where they will entrap the Utah warriors. Winnetou enrages the warriors by calling them effeminate saying that "Utah are old women. They follow Rolling Thunder who is a liar." However, in the end it is Big Wolf who kills Rolling Thunder, and he subsequently allies with Old Shatterhand's group.

Meanwhile, the bandits, who have beaten Old Shatterhand's group to the valley, have to construct a raft in order to get to the cave where the treasure is held, which takes time. When several of the leaders do make it to the cave, an elderly Native American man named the Big Bear is guarding the treasure. The bandits shoot him and go inside the cave to find the gold, but the leader of the bandits becomes overcome with greed and kills his companions. With his dying breath, the Big Bear grabs a chain just inside the cave, releasing a false floor in the room with the treasure, sending the bandits and the gold into a pit.

When the bandit leaders do not return from the cave, the rest of the bandits prepare to kill Fred and Ellen, who are still their hostages. Just as Fred is about to be hung, Old Shatterhand's group, with Big Wolf and the Utah warriors, arrive and free Fred and Ellen, and the Utah warriors kill the bandits (who it turns out were the ones who destroyed the village). The Utah and Old Shatterhand's group part ways happily, and Old Shatterhand and Winnetou ride off into the canyon alone together.

There are similarities between *Treasure of Silver Lake* and the US Westerns we examined earlier. Old Shatterhand and Winnetou are fairly stereotypical as resourceful and knowledgeable frontiersmen. Similar to younger male characters in *Red*

River, The Searchers, and *The Magnificent Seven*, it is Fred who is both hot-headed and who has the only love interest story line. However, there are also some interesting differences, most particularly in the character of the Duke of Glockenspiel, Karl Heinz Leopold Ulrich (Eddi Arent). The Duke appears as a type of comic relief: he is an avid butterfly hunter, who tends to be solely focused on finding rare butterflies to the exclusion of his surroundings, and even his name is a joke (a glockenspiel is a percussion instrument). He is also viewed as harmless and effeminate by the bandits, who dismiss him despite the fact that he can shoot well (which he proves in the final scene). At the same time, the Duke also serves as a contrast to the more obviously well-equipped Old Shatterhand, who is adept on the frontier while the Duke bumbles around. Finally, the Duke serves as verification that Old Shatterhand is bona fide even in "civilized" areas—when the Duke meets Old Shatterhand and Winnetou for the first time, he says that word of their fame had reached Vienna.

Like their US counterparts, the Winnetou films were immensely popular in West Germany, and (following the practice of American corporations for product spin-offs), they also sparked one of the first examples of movie merchandising there. Fans could buy a record of the soundtrack (with one song becoming the best-selling single on German music charts for fourteen weeks), board games, cookbooks, clothes, comic books, and hundreds of different toys.[18]

This merchandising fit in well with the West German hobbyists who played Indian in locations like the Munich Cowboy Club. After World War II, US military forces continued to occupy West Germany (in fact there are still US military bases in Germany today), and this kept American GIs there, some of whom were members of Native American tribes. US military leaders encouraged these men to build relationships with German hobbyists as a way to create connections across national lines and to make the US occupation of Germany seem more friendly than punitive.[19] One could find clubs, America Houses, and exhibitions showing indigenous artifacts in West German cities like Munich, Düsseldorf, Berlin, and Essen. These allowed West Germans to come into contact (at least superficially) with Native American culture enough so that it reinforced the mythic West created by writers such as Karl May

Drawing from the popularity of the Winnetou films in West Germany, in East Germany (GDR) the Deutsche Film-Aktiengesellschaft (DEFA, or the German Film Corporation) production company also took up the genre. However, their films also reflected the allegiance of the GDR with the USSR. For example, instead of calling the films "Westerns," which would focus on the West as a geographic place or on the "settlement" of the West by Euro-Americans, East German filmmakers and audiences called them *Indianerfilme*, or "films about Indians." Audiences were

---

18. Goral, *Cold War Rivalry*, 64.

19. Penny, *Kindred by Choice*, 204.

expected to sympathize with Native Americans as a rejection of what East German filmmakers saw as imperialist US capitalism, which robbed indigenous people of their land and commodified everything, including Indian scalps.[20] The DEFA attempted to focus on the generalized greed of corporations and the government instead of on individual settlers, farmers, or cowboys (who were largely absent from the films). Conflicts between Native Americans were minimized in the films, and hostilities between tribes were explained by white influence or manipulation.[21]

Like US Westerns and the West German Winnetou films, hundreds of thousands of East German people went to see Indianerfilme soon after they opened (they were not shown in West Germany or the US), and the films made a relatively hefty profit for the DEFA. They were also popular with GDR politicians. When almost all feature films (of any kind) were banned by the GDR authorities in 1965, the Indianerfilme titled *The Sons of Great Bear* was one of the few survivors.[22] Westerns as a genre were popular with GDR government authorities partly because they could be used to reinforce government-approved messages, and also because they were one of the few types of films that were reliably profitable.

While the Indianerfilme and the Karl May Westerns shared the same roots, we see the influence of the East German political context when we look at *Blood Brothers (Blutsbrüder)*, East Germany's most popular film from 1975. Here, a US Army soldier, nicknamed "Harmonica" (Dean Reed), deserts his unit with two other men. Harmonica is disturbed by the slaughter of Native American women and children by the army, while the other two men want to go find gold in Montana. The other two men, beat and kill several Native American women whom they come across washing clothes in a stream, and then run off. Harmonica saves the woman who has not been killed (Fawn, played by Gisela Freudenberg), and attempts to nurse her back to health, although she quickly escapes.

Fawn's tribe (the film does not specify which she is meant to be from) then captures Harmonica, and he is forced to compete with Fawn's brother, Hard Rock (Gojko Mitic), in a foot race and feats of strength. Being essentially a pacifist, Harmonica refuses to kill Hard Rock, even when Hard Rock is injured in a fall. Because the fight is a draw, and because Fawn pleads Harmonica's case, the chief allows Harmonica to live and settle with the tribe. Harmonica and Fawn fall in love, are married, and she becomes pregnant.

However, one day when Harmonica, Hard Rock, and the other men are out hunting, the US Army comes through the camp and kills everyone, sparking Harmonica's hunt for revenge. He stays on that path until he finds Fawn's killer, but loses heart when he sees the man greeted by a wife and child, instead

20. Goral, *Cold War Rivalry*, 94.

21. Birgel, "The Only Good Indian is a DEFA Indian," 48–49.

22. Birgel, "The Only Good Indian is a DEFA Indian," 57.

FIGURE 5.2 *Blood Brothers* movie poster (1975)
Source: Blutsbrüder. Original release East-German movie poster. DEFA, 1975.

empathizing with him via a series of flashbacks between himself and Fawn. Instead, Harmonica goes on a quest with Hard Rock to liberate Native Americans who are being rounded up by the Army and put on reservations.

Much like other DEFA films, *Blood Brothers* begins with American-born Dean Reed, who plays Harmonica, talking directly to the camera, declaring in German "This is a love song. This is a love film . . . about love for everyone. Love for a woman, for my wife in the film. Love for a new family, that in this film existed 100 years ago in America, and I'm in an Indian tribe, but it could be today in the GDR, or Argentina or Chile or in another country too. And love, for an ideal for freedom. For friendship between two friends, Gojko [Gojko Mitić who played the Native American character named *Harter Felsen* or Hard Rock] and me, in the film." The film then abruptly cuts away to Reed in a recording studio, singing in English "Love your brother! But hate . . . your enemy! I used to think that peace and love were just the same, then I learned that life is not only a game. Each man must fight, and fight again, but never, never, never let your life just flow away. Let your life have value every day." The song goes on to emphasize fighting for freedom against oppression. After the song concludes, the film returns briefly to Reed who says that although the film has a lot of action, it is primarily a film about love (a somewhat jarring contrast after the stridency of the song).

Reed's speech, the song, and the film all make for a lot to unpack. To do that we need to know a bit more about Reed himself, as he both starred in the film and cowrote the script. He was born in Colorado, went to Hollywood as a young man, and became an actor, at which he was moderately successful. He then went on to a music career, and was on tour in South America when he turned against US intervention in other nations. He went to Europe, even acting in some Italian Westerns before making tours of the USSR. While he was at a film festival in Leipzig he met the woman who would become his wife, and they settled in the GDR.

Reed was popular with East German and Eastern Bloc audiences both because he was "exotic" as an American and because he was politically valuable as someone who had publicly rejected the US. For Reed himself, films like *Blood Brothers* allowed him to make pointed political critiques against America's proxy wars like Vietnam, the CIA's covert operations in South America (hence the reference to Chile in the introduction to *Blood Brothers*), and the treatment of Native Americans within the US during the American Indian Movement in the 1970s (notably, members of AIM marched in East Berlin's May Day parades in the 1960s and 1970s).[23] In this Reed was not a pacifist, as attested to by both the "hate your enemy" in the opening song and the fact that *Blood Brothers* ends with Hard Rock and Harmonica essentially mounting a guerilla campaign against US forces.[24] Reed created yet another archetype of masculinity: being a man not only required protecting loved ones and family from harm, but also standing up to greedy political and military powers that took resources and land at the expense of less powerful groups.

Audiences and critics liked the message of *Blood Brothers*, and it, like the other Indianerfilme, was popular. East German *Berlin National Newspaper* (*Nationalzeitung Berlin*) described it as an "Indian film with a moral claim" and Reed himself was described in East German press as the "Red Sinatra."[25] By the time of *Blood Brothers*, Reed's Yugoslavian costar Gojko Mitić had already been a film star for many years. He was not only popular within East Germany—the first film celebrity in East German Cinema—but also in the Eastern Bloc countries generally.[26]

The Role of Women in Westerns

Up to this point I have focused on male characters, in large part because the films under discussion did. They celebrated heroic masculine qualities such as being violent when necessary, protecting home and family (particularly wives and daughters), coming together as well as being individualistic, and able to lead groups of men. What about the female characters? Scholars generally agree that the strong

---

23. Birgel, "The Only Good Indian is a DEFA Indian," 57.

24. Seán Allan, "Transnational Stardom: DEFA's Management of Dean Reed," in *Re-Imagining DEFA: East German Cinema in its National and Transnational Contexts*, ed. Seán Allan and Sebastian Heiduschke (New York: Berghahn, 2016).168–190.

25. Goral, *Cold War Rivalry*, 50.

26. Goral, *Cold War Rivalry*, 67.

development of male characters came at the expense of the way women were portrayed in the films. In the 1970s it was argued that women's roles in John Ford films were flat stereotypes, confined to mothering, burying, comforting, and feeding male characters; they did not seem to have lives of their own (even if they did have occasional moments of heroism).[27] More recently, professor of film and media studies Gaylyn Studlar has argued that while the female characters in Westerns that John Ford directed didn't escape US gender stereotypes of the mid twentieth century, they were in fact more developed—more human—than previous scholars have recognized.[28]

There is some evidence to support Studlar's claims. Female characters in Hollywood films such as *Red River* and *The Searchers* (as well as *Blood Brothers*), shows some complexity in feminine qualities. In *Red River*, the character of Tess bucks the stereotype of the helpless woman: when the wagon train is attacked by Indians, she defends it with a rifle. However, she does serve in a typical pacifist role of women when she breaks up the fight between Dunston and Garth.

White women's femininity plays an important role in *The Searchers* because the two girls have been abducted. While Edwards finds the elder girl's body (the implication is that she has been raped), the younger girl, Debbie, remains missing. Her fate drives the main tension between Edwards and Pawley; when they find Debbie, Edwards intends to kill her because she is presumed to have been sexually violated, and Pawley intends to stop him and take Debbie home.

These women's roles are an echo of the theme of anti–race-mixing that we have seen throughout this book, particularly in chapter 3 where French and British colonial officials tied white women's femininity to sexual purity, specifically vis-à-vis indigenous men. For Wayne's character in *The Searchers*, white women who have been living with the Comanche are no longer white. When Edwards and Pawley go to a fort where Native Americans have been captured by soldiers, they check several white women in the chapel to see if Debbie is among them. The film depicts these women as mentally ill as a result of their time with the Native Americans. When Pawley says that "it's hard to believe they're white," Edwards replies, "they aren't white. They're Comanche now."

The tensions between race and femininity—and the relationship to sexual purity—is particularly evident in *The Searchers* when the character Laurie Jorgenson (Vera Miles) gives a speech to Pawley. Laurie advises Pawley to kill Debbie, while Pawley rejects bloodshed in favor of compassion. In the scene, Jorgensen (wearing her white wedding dress, a symbol of sexual purity) says to Pawley when he talks about rescuing Debbie: "Fetch what home? The leavings of Comanche bucks sold time and again to the highest bidder?" She tells Pawley

---

27. Michael Dempsey, "John Ford: A Reassessment," *Film Quarterly* 28, no. 4 (1975): 2–15, 7.

28. Gaylyn Studlar, "2: Sacred Duties, Poetic Passions: John Ford and the Issue of Femininity in the Western," in *John Ford Made Westerns: Film the Legend in the Sound Era*, ed. Gaylyn Studlar and Matthew Bernstein (Bloomington: Indiana University Press, 2001), 43–74.

that Martha (Debbie's mother) would want Edwards to "put a bullet in her brain." This moment is also telling because racial and gender norms intersect—by urging Pawley to kill Debbie, Jorgensen is enforcing a patriarchy in which (white) men have control over women's bodies.[29] For Laurie, Debbie's potential sexual impurity marks her as being outside the bounds of white women's femininity—sex outside of Christian marriage (consensual or not) being one of the differences between white civilized femininity and nonwhite, "savage" femininity.

German filmmakers expanded on roles for women beyond the limited ones in John Ford's Westerns and the *Red River*. In the *Treasure of Silver Lake*, the character of Ellen (Fred's love interest) tends to follow the example of women in most US Westerns, serving as a compassionate counterpart to her young suitor. However, Mrs. Butler (the widow) is formidable in mounting a defense of her homestead—a fact that one of the male characters remarks upon, proclaiming "you're a hellofa woman!"

However, it was the East German Indianerfilme that portrayed women—particularly Native American women—in perhaps the most nuanced manner. Whereas in many Westerns Native American women served as sexual objects (for example, being shown partly nude while bathing), in *Blutsbrüder* Fawn is more than a love interest, serving as a connection to her community. When she attempts to save Harmonica from being killed, it is because she recognizes him as an honorable man, believes in justice, and is able to identify the murderers, not because she loves him (that comes later).[30] Her death also serves as the break-up of community, both in the sense that the Indian village is wiped out and in that it causes Harmonica to break permanently with the white community, instead retreating into violence by seeking revenge for her death.

Conclusion

In this chapter we have focused on the ways that Westerns in the US and in West and East Germany portrayed gender—predominantly masculinity as reflected by Cold War politics. While US films from the 1940s and 1950s, such as *Red River* and the *Searchers* portrayed masculinity in more complex ways, they still generally supported the overall self-image that the US was constructing during the Cold War: that the nation was a strong world leader, able to forge a path through "uncivilized" or empty territory (whether that be the mythic West of the 1800s or the new frontier of space in the 1960s).

---

29. Studlar, "2: Sacred Duties, Poetic Passions," 54.

30. Heidi Denzel de Tirado, "6—Interracial Romance, Taboo, and Desire in the Eastern Counter-Western Blutsbrüder," in *Gender and Sexuality in East German Film: Intimacy and Alienation*, ed. Kyle Frackman and Faye Stewart (Cambridge: Cambridge University Press, 2018), 126–145.

136 ROOTS OF CONTEMPORARY ISSUES

In contrast to this, creators of the Winnetou films in West Germany used the masculinity of Karl May's characters to argue for a more racially inclusive notion of the US West, even as they had to address the ways Nazis had used May's works. The East German Indianerfilme projected a third type of masculinity, in which Native Americans and those sympathetic to them were the heroes, in a deliberate critique of what GDR leaders saw as American capitalist imperialism.

It is also notable here that rather than serving as a metropole, in this chapter Europe serves as a recipient of US influence and "soft power." In some ways, this marks the end of European imperial power—those who were once the colonizers are now the colonized. As tempting as such a conclusion would be, it is also far too simplistic. As we saw within the genre of Westerns in literature and films, the US and Europe had been in dialogue with one another for hundreds of years. At the same time, however, the imagined space of Westerns, as an empty and mythic "frontier" of the past, allowed both US and European (in the case study of this chapter, East and West German), to project their own political and gendered meanings.

FURTHER READING

Corkin, Stanley. *Cowboys as Cold Warriors: The Western and U.S. History*. Philadelphia: Temple University Press, 2004.

Miller, Cynthia J., and A. Bowdoin Van Ripper, eds. *International Westerns: Re-Locating the Frontier*. Lanham, MD: Scarecrow Press, 2014.

Penny, H. Glen. *Kindred by Choice: Germans and American Indians since 1800*. Chapel Hill: University of North Carolina Press, 2013.

Poiger, Uta G. "A New, 'Western' Hero? Reconstructing German Masculinity in the 1950s." *Signs* 24, no. 1 (Autumn 1998): 147–62.

Rydell, Robert W. *Buffalo Bill in Bologna: The Americanization of the World, 1869–1922*. Chicago: University of Chicago Press, 2005.

Shaw, Tony, and Denise J. Youngblood. *Cinematic Cold War: The American and Soviet Struggle for Hearts and Minds*. Lawrence: University Press of Kansas, 2010.

CONCLUSION

A Postgender World?

I began this volume by making the argument that gender is a complex system, composed of many different levels of choices and structures. Because gender is an imbedded part of our culture, it is difficult to see the ways in which it functions. We therefore had to look at moments of contact and change, when people used gender as a way to exercise or resist the political authority of imperialism. We consequently looked at the ways that the expansion of European empires overseas shaped the spread of European gender norms. At the same time, we've also seen the ways in which colonized people resisted, adapted, and used gender norms to question the imposition of European political power and to argue for self-rule. We have also examined different types of sources in order to reveal the spread of these ideas—laws and religious texts, commodities, spaces, clothing, and films. This was partly a pragmatic choice on my part, as a way to narrow down a huge topic into a book-sized argument, but it also allowed us to focus on the role that different sources can play in historical analysis. In other words, just like today, people in the past existed in a multifaceted reality, and we can use different types of sources to illuminate their world.

By now you should have not only gained an understanding of the ways that people have constructed gender in the past, but also begun to see new insights into how *you* construct your own gender and how you perceive the gender of those around you. My goal is that you can then take this new lens—a new way of looking at the world—and see the implications of gender more broadly in areas such as politics, culture, and economics.

Your gender—both the ways that you perceive it and the ways that other people perceive you—has shaped who you are and our society at large. Your task now is to decide the ways in which it will shape your individual future and those of the society you live in. How will you construct your appearance? How will you structure your household living arrangements? What types of governmental policies will you support on issues such as paternal and maternal family leave? What about women in leadership positions? How will gender shape your economic life—the type of work you do, the things you buy, and so on? How do the characters in the books you read and the TV and films that you watch construct and enact ideas of gender? The answers to these questions will determine the ways in which we organize our lives around gender norms in the future—which traits we decide are masculine, feminine, both, or other, and what implications that has for our society.

As we conclude our discussion, there are a few areas that you may want to research if you are interested in exploring the ways that gender shaped imperialism and vice versa (although you probably aren't going to write a book!). You can use the questions that I asked you consider in the preceding paragraph to begin to think about a contemporary aspect of gender norms as they relate to imperialism, or more broadly to political power and influence. The Pew Research Center might be a good place to start for information about today—they have a whole section on the topic of gender.[1] As you do your research, be sure that you continue to be aware that gender encompasses masculinity, femininity, and nonbinary alternatives (many organizations and news sites have tended to incorrectly use "gender" when they mean "women").

Once you have the contemporary issue, there are a few different directions that you could go in for further research. You can use the following questions as a base to start your explorations; once you get a little bit farther into your research, you can formulate a question that reflects your specific interest in the topic:

> How did gender norms shape the experience of contact between different cultures? We focused on the Spanish in Mexico and Peru, but you could consider:
> - Contact between indigenous people and the French and British fur trade in North America from the 1600s to the 1800s; British, Dutch, and French in the Pacific Islands in the 1700s and 1800s; or Europeans in Africa during the late 1800s.
>
> What was the role of gender in economic systems? We looked at the role of gender in the transatlantic slave trade during the seventeenth and eighteenth centuries, and focused on Jamaica and sugar plantations. However, you might want to consider:
> - The different roles that gender played in societies in other industries, such as mining areas like Minas Gerais in Brazil, tobacco farms in the United States, or cotton plantations in the US South.
> - The lives of urban slaves, who were more likely to engage in craft work and domestic service.
> - Other empires, such as the Portuguese and French empires in the Atlantic, which make for good comparisons to our case study of the British Empire.

---

1. Pew Research Center, Topic: gender, https://www.pewresearch.org/topics/gender/. Accessed August 28, 2020.

- Going beyond the time period and European empires to look at the ways that different economic systems such as capitalism and communism influenced gender roles, such as in Communist China during the middle of the twentieth century.

What role did gender play in European settlement of colonized areas? We examined the case of the French in Algeria and Indochina during the nineteenth and early twentieth century, but you might want to consider researching:

- The Western United States, Western Canada, Australia, or South Africa, all of which had large influxes of Europeans who intended to permanently settle in the area. They brought with them ideas of gender norms, but then had to adapt when they were on the ground in those areas. In this process they also impacted indigenous gender norms, partly because Europeans disrupted indigenous society by forcing them to migrate from their traditional geographic areas.
- Going beyond European empires to examine gender and Russian colonization of Central Asia. Much like in the United States, Russian officials relocated indigenous peoples and created incentives for Russians to settle on the land.

What ways were nationalist movements gendered? We studied these movements in India and Egypt by looking at clothing. You could also explore the ways that gender influenced:

- Specific areas of politics and society, such as voting rights (who gets to be involved in the government), legal rights (how someone is treated by others), and economic rights (such as the ability to own and inherit property, and the right to earn wages). You could explore these issues in the United States or France during the late 1700s and early 1800s.
- Going beyond European colonies, you could look at China during the Revolution, Great Leap Forward, and Cultural Revolution, or Central Asia during the Soviet period.
- If you are interested in art, you might want to consider the roles of gendered symbols in nationalist movements. A good place to start with this topic is "mother India," but you could also look at Marianne (France), John Bull and Britannia (Britain), or Uncle Sam and Miss Columbia (United States).

What role did gender play in the Cold War? We explored the role of film (particularly Westerns) and the ways that these reflected their Cold War context. You could also:

- Consider the role of women in Cold War anticolonial movements, such as Algerian women in the Algerian Revolution during the 1950s and 1960s, the Vietnam War in the 1950s to the 1970s, Nicaragua in the 1960s, Cuba in the 1950s, Mexico during the early 1900s, Iran in the 1970s and 1980s, or Liberia in the 1990s.

- Explore the role of gender in political and cultural movements in Latin America. As US media spread during the Cold War it became highly politicized in countries such as Brazil, Argentina, Chile, and Mexico. Things that we would not consider political (such as listening to certain types of music, wearing some types of clothing, and having some hairstyles) were deeply charged, and could get young people arrested and killed.

These are some general topics and areas to start your research, but be aware that your focus will likely change over time, depending on what sources you find on your topic. You can often begin getting a general sense of your topic by looking at an encyclopedia, or an online resource such as Wikipedia (however, be sure to use nonscholarly sources with caution; the people writing the information may not be experts, and you should verify the information that you gather from them as soon as you find scholarly sources). I generally begin with a list of five or six proper nouns—persons or events that are important to my topic. In addition, it's helpful to establish a basic chronology of five to seven events for your topic. Finally, you'll want some synonyms; a thesaurus is helpful here, or a dictionary. When looking for primary sources on your topic, it's also helpful to identify the terms that people who lived during the time period you are researching would have used. Remember that these may be different from ones that we use today, and we may now consider them derogatory or offensive (remember our discussion of two-spirit vs. berdache from chapter 1).

Having a list of proper nouns, dates, and synonyms will help you as you do your research. As I stated in the introduction, I begin looking for sources in my university's library catalog. I enter the terms that I think are useful, and I almost always add "history" to them. You may have to try different combinations before you find a term that works. Don't be discouraged! Research takes time, and sometimes you'll find a great resource on the third, fourth, or fifth page of your results. Once you find a source that you think is relevant, be sure to check the other sources that have been identified by the Library of Congress librarians as being on that same topic. Your library catalog may call these "topics" or "subjects," and they may be hyperlinks. It's very likely that examining these lists will lead you to incredibly useful sources. And finally, once you find a book or article, don't forget to check out their footnotes and bibliography—take advantage of the research that the author has already done! Taking your time and being through with each of these steps should ensure that you have a successful research process and set you up very well to begin to write on your topic. Good luck and have fun!

INDEX

ABOUT THE COVER

In 1770, the Italian-born painter Agostino Brunias (c. 1730–1796) sailed to the Caribbean, where he made his career as a colonial painter. Brunias's paintings offer romanticized images of slavery, generally portraying the conditions of slaves as better than they were, for example by showing slaves in leisure activities instead of working in the fields. However, he also depicted black and mixed-race subjects with a dignity and reverence rarely seen in European art at that time. In *Linen Day, Roseau, Dominica—A Market Scene* (1770), Brunias shows well-to-do-whites, free persons of color, and enslaved people mingling in a weekly market. The clothing worn by the subjects in the painting is finely detailed. In the painting, free people of African origin wear the same types of European fashions as the whites, including the head wrap. There is a hierarchy within the enslaved subjects in the painting, as revealed by their clothing—the less clothing that the person has on, the lower their status. Throughout the Caribbean, markets such as this one were dynamic sites of economic and social exchange where colorful textiles could be acquired and enslaved persons could participate as both buyers and sellers in global trade networks.